More Writer's First Aid:

Getting the Writing Done

BOOK TWO

Kristi Holl

Writer's Institute
Publications

www.WritersInstitutePublications.com

About the Author

Kristi Holl is an award-winning author of over 40 books for children, two nonfiction books for writers, and over 250 stories and articles for children and adults. She taught writing for the Institute of Children's Literature for 25 years. She now spends the majority of her time writing books and speaking at writers' conferences. Kristi started as an elementary teacher and began writing as a hobby when staying home with her children. Kristi has always combined writing with parenting; personal experiences figure prominently in her magazine stories and articles, as well as her books.

Design and Production Editor

Joanna Horvath

Illustrations supplied by iStockphoto

International Standard Book Number 978-1-889715-63-6

1-800-443-6078. www.WritersBookstore.com
E-mail:Services@WritersBookstore.com

Contents

IV. Family Matters

A Word from the Author

You won't actually find bandages or medicine in *More Writer's First Aid*. But in 48 chapters, you will find cures for dealing with disappointment and jealousy, writing despite physical and emotional pain, banishing procrastination once and for all, and combining writing with parenting (from infancy to adulthood). "We're all in this together," has been my motto for many years.

I've had over 40 books published in 30 years of writing, taught writing for more than 25 years, and have guided, mentored, and taught hundreds of aspiring writers. I started writing on an Iowa farm, very isolated, with no Internet and no other writers around. It's *not* about how talented you are—and it's *not* who you know—that gets you published. Most often the published writers are simply those writers who refused to quit. I can help you persevere until you publish.

—Kristi Holl

Enjoying the Writing Life— Every Day!

What Kind of Boss Are You?

"I want to be my own boss."

That statement is often made by people who want to quit their day jobs and work at home. As writers, we love the idea of no one telling us what to do. We love being able to schedule our work and our days. It's a wonderful system—but only if you have a wonderful boss.

Are you the kind of boss *you'd* like to work for? Many days I am, but it's taken years to get to this point. Over the years I've been many kinds of bosses—some of them good, some destructive. Which kind are *you*?

The Coach Boss

In my early years of writing, back when it was all new to me, my boss was a real coach. Enthusiastic, fun, excited, non-restrictive. She wanted me to explore all my writing and publishing options, try various topics and formats just to see if I liked them, and she never harped about the bottom line.

She was fun to work for—and my work showed it (in terms of both quantity and quality)—despite being surrounded by babies and toddlers at the time.

The Authoritarian Boss

I worked for this boss next. He held a whip over my head, which he cracked often (e.g., if I slowed down or considered taking a sick day). To be honest, this boss got a LOT of work out of me. I dragged myself to his office no matter how sick I was. Days off were frowned on, so I rarely took one.

It wasn't worth it anyway. I felt his condemning glare no matter where I tried to hide from him. It was easier to give in and work nonstop than fight him. After all, there were bills to pay! I knew the quality of my writing was going down, but this boss didn't seem to notice or care. Quantity was everything to him.

The Paranoid Boss
This boss believed in lots of networking, and at first, I liked his ideas. I met other writers, read their work, saw their websites, blogs, podcasts, newsletters, and webinars, YouTube videos and book trailers. Unfortunately, my boss couldn't let me enjoy all the new things I was seeing.

He started breathing down my neck, changing orders every half hour. "We're behind the times!" he'd whisper in my ear. "Create a newsletter!" I'd start that project, but soon he said, "Yours isn't as good as the competition's! Drop that and create a teleseminar instead!" No matter how many projects I juggled, this boss let me know it was never good enough. My job was always in jeopardy. I took out stock in an antacid company.

The Dream Boss
While I was in the hospital recovering from working for the paranoid boss, a wonderful thing happened. My dream boss visited one day with a bouquet of daffodils and box of chocolates—and offered me a job. I've been working for this boss ever since, and I hope she lives forever!

She gives me one project to do at a time. "Multi-tasking is another name for fragmented," she informed me. I now write for two hours before I'm required to do anything else.

My boss doesn't compare my work to anyone else's. She loves quality, but she doesn't measure quality by the size of the advance.

My boss is understanding about sick days, yet she makes sure I show up for work most of the time because she knows I'm happier that way.

You're the Boss!

Writers are in the enviable position of being their own bosses. Are you the kind of boss you'd like to work for?

If not, you have the power to change that. Starting today, be your ideal boss. List the traits of your perfect boss, the kind of treatment you'd love to receive. Then turn around and give yourself that treatment. You'll be a happier, more productive employee!

Honoring the Writing Process

Writers are frequently advised, "You have to honor the process." What does that mean exactly?

Every piece of new writing is a voyage into the unknown. There are things you can do that help (or honor) the writing process— many things! There are just as many that sabotage (or dishonor) the writing process.

You have to accept the complexity of writing, how it comes together for you, and what you need in order to nurture the process. Simple example: If you know you need seven hours of sleep in order to write well the next morning, you honor the process when you go to bed early enough to sleep those hours. You dishonor your writing process by staying up till all hours and arriving at the keyboard the next morning in a fog.

Ways You Dishonor the Process

There are many ways we unknowingly and accidentally dishonor the writing process. We may:

- get a great idea for a story, but wait until we have time later to write it down, and when "later" comes, we can't remember it.
- rush into writing a rough draft before we've given the idea time to "cook."
- have habits detrimental to our health.
- have such critical voices in our heads that everything we write sounds like rubbish, so we give up in discouragement.

We all probably dishonor our writing process in different ways, depending on our personalities and backgrounds.

Ways You Honor the Process

If you wanted to honor the writing process, you might:

- keep a pen and notebook handy to jot down ideas immediately.
- let your idea grow and simmer before starting the rough draft.
- eat good "brain" food, get enough exercise, and do what's needed to avoid injuries from sitting all day.
- do whatever's necessary to silence the negative voices (e.g., pray, do positive self-talk, read motivational books, see a counselor).

In *Deep Writing*, author Eric Maisel made this observation: "I hope that you'll take seriously the notion that you can help or harm the writing process and that, in a corner of awareness, you already know which of the two you are doing . . . When you find the courage to explore your own truth about honoring and dishonoring the process, some writing successes are bound to happen."

What about you? Have you thought about this? In what ways do you dishonor the writing process? How can you work activities or behaviors into your life that would honor the process instead?

Get out your journal and start making two lists. Then, one by one, eliminate the **dishonor**ing activities and add the **honor**ing activities to your day. Over time, what a change you will see!

Dealing with Disappointment

Disappointments come in all shapes and sizes, and they can thoroughly derail our urge to write. The disappointments might be writing related (like a dismal writing session, or receiving a rejection). Non-writing disappointments also impact our ability to focus and be creative (the loss of a friendship, your child in trouble at school again, something doesn't turn out the way you had hoped).

A cloud hovers over us. Spirits droop. How can we keep writing after experiencing a disappointment?

First of all, we can stop waiting for the magical day when disappointments no longer occur. Occasional letdowns and dashed hopes are a fact of life. They will come. Our only choice is in how we respond. Will we let them dampen our creativity and destroy our writing days? Or will we turn the disappointment into an opportunity for growth?

Adjust Reality

Many disappointments occur (with the accompanying stress) because of the gap between your expectations and reality. When you have an expectation about the way something should happen and then reality falls short of that expectation, it creates a disappointment that in turn breeds stress. For example, you expected to finish that rough draft today, but couldn't because you had to take your child to the dentist, your mom to the doctor, and your dog to the vet. You're frustrated and disappointed at the end of the day.

In this case, an easy way to avoid such disappointment is to bring reality more in line with your expectations. Look at your calendar, and plan your day the night before.

Don't just have a vague idea in the back of your mind that you'll "write that story tomorrow." Instead, make up a "to do" list each night for the next day. Include not only the things you have to do, but, just as important, the things you want to do. Prioritize them in order of their importance, and put writing near the top. You'll experience much less disappointment if you don't set yourself up with false expectations.

Delay or Suspend Judgment

Many disappointments are totally out of our control. They just happen. Someone doesn't show up on time—or at all. The story or book that an editor was so excited about gets rejected after nine months. Our department at work is down-sized and our income shrinks along with it. You hear that a grown sibling or neighbor has spread nasty, untrue rumors about you. Whatever the disappointment is, don't be too quick to judge the person's conduct (or the apparent conduct of the person) who has disappointed you. Often what we see is not what is truly going on.

We usually don't understand why this person is behaving in this manner (even though we think we do). We seldom have all the facts of the situation. So choose to suspend judgment and criticism until a later time. *When a disappointment occurs, assume you don't know all the facts or extenuating circumstances.* Ninety-nine percent of the time, your assumption will be accurate. Delay any judging and criticizing or reacting till you know the facts—just put a lid on it for now. This will go a long way toward staying calm and being able to think and write.

Take Time to Think

Our initial reaction to a disappointing situation—what comes naturally to most of us—may not be the best response. In fact, if you don't take time to think (or better yet, sleep on it and pray for perspective and wisdom) your reaction can cause a whole string of further (and worse) regrets to deal with. Every one of these overblown reactions will rob you of writing energy. Count on it!

We've all seen and participated in not-so-serious discussions that erupted into angry fights, multiplying the stressful event tenfold. Oftentimes, when the dust has settled and a calm discussion of the event takes place days later, misunderstandings are apparent on

both sides. So don't allow a disappointment—no matter its size—
to escalate.

> **Be Verbal!**
> Unspoken expectations also come into play. Before you react
> negatively to a disappointment ("Why couldn't he keep the
> kids out of my hair just one hour today so I could write?"),
> be sure that you actually verbalized your hopes or expecta-
> tions. No one is a good mind reader. If you didn't ask your
> husband to keep the kids out of your hair so you could
> write, you can't assume that he knows they're bothering you
> or that you have trouble writing with a million interruptions.
>   He's used to watching you cook, clean, garden and drive
> carpool while handling umpteen questions from little ones.
> *He may not know, without being told, that your writing is
> different and needs peace and quiet.* Don't set yourself up
> for disappointment—and a ruined weekend—because you
> didn't speak up and then got angry because he didn't read
> your mind.

Trust Your Calm Inner Response

Settle down, then look inside yourself for your adult response. The
little kid in you has had his day and internally ranted and raved,
but the grown-up in you usually knows the best course of action
to take, if you'll just listen to him.

The adult response may not be what we want to hear. The child in
us wants to respond in retaliation to a perceived hurt or outright
attack on our writing or some other aspect of our life. Retaliating
rarely helps, no matter how much your loyal best friend urges you
"not to take that lying down!" Ranting, raving, and seeking
revenge wastes an extraordinary amount of writing energy—and
time!

If you'll listen, your calmer inner adult will know—and tell you—
how to respond appropriately without starting World War III.
Respond to the disappointment in a manner that is also best for the
other person. How? Without accusation or causing embarrassment
to the other person, and without seeking any kind of revenge.

People will disappoint us, sometimes quite badly. None of us is perfect. The disappointment for you will lift—along with the writing doldrums—if you can follow this advice. (Please understand that I'm talking about disappointments here, not truly abusive situations. You do not overlook abuse.)

Battlefield of the Mind

Last, don't focus on the hurt or the person or the disappointment. Literally remove your mind from the subject. Shove it to the back burner for now. Dwelling on the rejection or bad review will magnify it, and thus magnify your pain, and prolong your writing block or lethargy.

If you must think about it—if the situation demands attention—then search for a silver lining. See what the disappointment can teach you, or how you can stretch and grow because of it. Did the rejection or review give you ideas for improvement? Pull out whatever constructive advice you can find. Don't just focus on the disappointment itself. Look beyond it.

"This too shall pass," and it will pass faster if you don't concentrate on it. Shift your mental gears. In the meantime—while you cool down and relax—you can also get a lot of writing done.

Striving for Contentment

Would you call yourself a *contented writer*? Are you happy with your current situation and writing progress?

Or are you a *dissatisfied writer*, striving to better yourself and always pushing hard toward your goals?

Embrace Opposite Traits

To be honest, if you want to enjoy the writing life—if you want to enjoy the process, and not just the final product—you'll have to find a way to embrace *both* contentment with your current progress and the urge to grow and improve. Why? *Because BOTH traits are important to your well-being as a writer and directly influence your career.*

At Peace with Writing

You need to be grateful for what you've learned as a writer. If you're a student, or you've been writing on your own for several months or years, take a look at your earliest stories and articles. You'll groan, or maybe grin, at what you considered great writing back then. You'll see how much you've learned about the craft of writing as well as the business of publishing. You can be grateful that your skills aren't what they used to be!

Giving yourself credit for how far you've come is important in keeping your spirits up. We melancholy writers are too quick to get down on ourselves, our abilities, our ideas, and our publishing record. This critical mind of ours (so very valuable during the editing process) can also be our greatest enemy if we don't "think about what we're thinking about."

It's probably true that you aren't where you want to be as a writer (I'm not either!), but be thankful that you're not back at the beginning. Note your progress with writing skills, marketing skills, how deeply you read, your new blog, and how your lessons are improving. Think about these *true, positive* things in your writing life. This is being *content* as a writer. It will allow you to enjoy the writing process.

Caution: Don't confuse being *content* with being *complacent*. A complacent attitude says, "I've arrived. You can't teach me anything. I can coast from now on." A complacent writer stops reading and studying and working at his craft the minute he emails his final lesson or makes his first big sale. Complacency keeps you stuck in one spot—and eventually you start sliding backwards.

Striving to Grow

The opposite of being content is the desire to mature in your writing, along with the inner gumption to press forward and make it happen. It's being consistent in your learning curve. By consistency, I mean devoting a certain amount of time almost daily to your writing growth. Maybe it's thirty minutes of reading writers' blogs or writing magazines. Maybe it's studying a good writing craft book. If you haven't set any writing goals for the year, it's not too late to do so. If you did set goals, re-visit them. See how you're doing.

> **Juggling Act**
> Like so many things in life, you have to find the balance. You want to enjoy your progress while *at the same time* moving forward in your goals. Don't go to the other extreme though. While you want to have enough "dissatisfied drive" to make steady progress in your career—you don't want to be *driven. Drive* is good, but being *driven* is no fun. It comes with ulcers and headaches. Learn how to maintain the necessary tension between these two points.

One of my favorite speakers has a saying: "I'm not where I want to be, but thank heavens I'm not where I used to be." She appreciates how far she's come. She's a happy woman who's content with her progress. But *at the same time* she also has her eye on a finish line further down the road.

Strive in your writing life for this perfect balance. You'll enjoy your current writing life on the way to where you're going!

Breaking the Procrastination Cycle

There's more to dealing with procrastination than snarling at yourself to "just do it!" I know because I've been snarling that line at myself for long periods. Sometimes I feel like snarling at everybody else too! I'm caught in the procrastination trap and trying to get out.

Did you know procrastination is a cycle with predictable stages? It isn't just one feeling with one cause. That's the bad news. I think the good news is that you can interrupt that cycle. The "how-to" depends on what part of the cycle you're in.

Stages of Procrastination

"The cycle starts with the pressure of being overwhelmed and ends with an attempt to escape through procrastination," says Neil Fiore in *The Now Habit: A Strategic Program for Overcoming Procrastination and Enjoying Guilt-Free Play.* "As long as you're caught in the cycle, there is no escape."

The vicious cycle of putting things off goes like this:

- starts with feeling overwhelmed
- pressure mounts
- we fear failing at whatever we're putting off
- we buckle down and try harder
- we work longer hours

- we feel resentful
- we get tired and lose motivation
- and *then we procrastinate.*

Wow! I always thought the "buckle down and try harder" and "work longer hours" part was good! It's how I've survived all these years. I certainly never considered it to be part of a procrastination habit or cycle—but the cycle signs ring true.

Warning Signs of Procrastination

"But I don't procrastinate," you may say. Maybe. Maybe not. As I read through the list of thirty-five symptoms in Dr. Fiore's book, I realized with great shock that I responded *yes* to about three-fourths of the questions! (It was a shock because for thirty years, people have told me what a hard worker I was, how organized I was, etc. And I'm quite productive.) But I had not considered certain behaviors as symptoms of procrastination.

Things like . . .

- Do you keep an impossibly long "to do" list?
- Do you talk to yourself in "shoulds"?
- Are you often late arriving at meetings and dinners?
- Do you have difficulty knowing what you really WANT for yourself, but are clear about what you SHOULD want?
- Do you find that you're never satisfied with what you accomplish?
- Do you feel deprived—either always working or feeling guilty about not working?
- Do you demand perfection even on low-priority work?
- Do you feel ineffective in controlling your life?

In my book *Writer's First Aid*, I maintained that you can't find a solution to a writing problem until you've correctly identified the problem, and then the root cause. If someone had told me that I was a procrastinator, I would have laughed out loud—until recently. But I have to admit that the questions hit home, and I definitely recognize that cycle of feelings!

Could it be that the burn-out I've felt this year comes from a life lived in the vicious procrastination cycle? If so, I want off that merry-go-round! I bet you do too.

Five Stages of Procrastination

According to Neil Fiore in *The Now Habit*, procrastination is similar to a situation where we scare ourselves into a frozen state. Fiore says to imagine a very long flat board on the ground in front of you, and then imagine walking on it to the other end of the board. Piece of cake, right?

Then he says imagine raising that board 100 feet off the ground, reaching from one tall building to another. Imagine walking across it again. You don't skip light-heartedly across now, do you? You worry about falling to your death—and you don't even take one step.

Then, in the third scenario, he says to imagine you smell smoke and feel heat on your back. You turn, and the building you stand on is in flames. You'll die if you don't get moving. What do you do now? Without even thinking, you get across that board. You might crawl, you might sit down and scooch across, but you get across to avoid being burned to a crisp.

That's procrastination in a nutshell. Here's how:

Five Predictable Stages

1) **You let a task determine your self-worth.** You think being successful at this task or goal will make you happy. You think your self-worth as a writer is wrapped up in this project.
2) **You use perfectionism to raise the task 100 feet above the ground**—like the imaginary board above. *"You demand that you do it perfectly—without anxiety, with complete acceptance from your audience, with no criticism,"* says Fiore.
3) **You find yourself frozen with anxiety.** Your imaginary difficulties with the project raise your stress level. Adrenaline kicks in. You seek temporary relief.
4) **You use procrastination to escape your self-created dilemma.** This brings the deadline closer and creates more pressure. You delay starting so long that you can't really be tested on your actual writing ability (what you are capable of if you'd started sooner).
5) **You use a real threat to jar you loose from the perfectionism and motivate yourself to begin.** The deadline, fast approaching, acts as the fire in the building. It forces you to get moving and actually begin the writing.

Breaking the Cycle

Fiore, in his terrific book then takes you back to the top of that tall building and asks you to imagine still being frozen as you face walking across that board. He says to imagine NO fire, but instead a strong, supportive net just three feet beneath the board. It will catch you if you fall. It stretches all the way to the other building. *There is no danger.* In that case, you would simply walk across. No problem. No threat.

The threats to our self-esteem (the deathly drop and the raging fire behind us) are self-created. That's actually good news because it means we have control over them. Safety nets are also self-created. That's more good news! You **can** break out of the vicious cycle of procrastination.

Your job, as the writer and protector of your psychological health, is to create such a safety net for yourself so you can approach your writing and begin with ease. You'll find other articles in *More Writer's First Aid*—especially those in Section 3 on "A Writer's Emotions"— that will help you create a safer writing environment.

How Tight Is Your Bow?

For ten straight days after returning from a dream vacation in England, I didn't sleep more than three or four hours per night. At first I thought it was severe jet lag, but as the days passed, I realized it was something else. I came home to a pile of work, multiple appointments, and various deadlines. When I awoke at 2 a.m., my mind was already racing about what to tackle first.

Wound Up or Winding Down?

One good thing that came from the insomnia is that I finished a terrific book, *The Relief of Imperfection* by Joan C. Webb. Near the end, she admitted, "Even after many years of more relaxed thinking and behavior, I still sometimes wonder how I'll accomplish my goals if I let up."

I know that other writers wonder the same thing. My students wonder about it—from the young moms to the retired teachers. My writer friends wonder about it. If we slow down—if we try to live a more balanced life—can we get it all done? Is it really possible?

Get Your Spring Back

Webb uses a great story in her book to illustrate her belief that unwinding and relaxing and slowing down can actually make you *more effective* in your work. This is the legend:

One morning a hunter stumbled over a man seated

> under a tree and playing with a small tame bird. "Why, you're
> the apostle John," exclaimed the hunter. "I'm surprised that
> an important and dedicated man like you would be out wast-
> ing your time."
>
> John looked up at the tall stranger and asked, "Why have
> you left that bow dangling on your shoulder?"
>
> "Well, don't you know?" replied the hunter. "If I kept it
> continually pulled tight, it would lose its spring and become
> ineffective."
>
> John chuckled and said, "That's the reason I play with
> this bird."

That really struck a chord with me—I knew I was continually
pulled tight inside. I had definitely lost my "spring" and was
becoming ineffective.

What about you? Is your bow continually tight? Are you afraid to
let it go slack for a while? I thought about that illustration for a
couple of days, then decided to try an experiment.

Loosen Up

Over Memorial Day weekend, I worked a bit, rested a bit, rode my
bike a bit, worked a bit more, played a bit, ate healthier food, and
"left the bow dangling on my shoulder" periodically. The result? I
got some office work done, but more importantly, I finally
unwound. Saturday night I slept *nine hours*.

Instead of jumping back into bad habits on Monday (my usual pattern), I continued the following week to keep my bow slack from
time to time throughout the day. I was astounded at the improvement in how I felt. I wasn't accomplishing quite as much writing
and marketing each individual day, but I eliminated the headaches
and back pain. It all eventually got done though—and the quality
was actually *better*.

How About You?

Stop and take a moment to assess the tightness of your own bow
today. Giving it a bit of slack *now* might very well help you hit that
bull's-eye *later*.

Joining a Work in Progress

One piece of advice new writers often hear is to "join a critique group!" They're immensely valuable in today's publishing climate where editors have so little time to edit and shape manuscripts.

You may be fortunate to find a group with an opening and be invited to join. Unless you're prepared, however, your critique group experience can be useless or even painful. If you step on enough toes, you could be asked to leave the group. To avoid that, follow these tips so you can join a critique group already in progress—and make it work for you.

Group in Progress
When you join a critique group in progress, you're joining an established "family." The group itself is a growing thing, and adding you to the group changes the dynamics. You, the new kid on the block, need to fit in without creating unnecessary disruption for the group. *Remember: the group has been functioning very well without you, and you're not there to revamp it.*

First, Don't Assume Anything.

Ask what length your manuscript should be for the sessions. In one new group I joined, I assumed (for some reason) that about 2,000 words (or a book chapter) would be a good length. I emailed the manuscript to each member a week before the scheduled meeting, as requested.

Within a few days, I was surprised to receive from the other members manuscripts closer to 500-600 words. I had unknowingly asked them to spend four times as long critiquing my work as everyone else's. I was embarrassed, and some of the members were put out.

Also, don't assume you should (or should not) bring a manuscript for critiquing at the first meeting. At one group I did not bring a manuscript the first time, thinking I hadn't yet "earned the right," and was told in no uncertain terms that I wasn't allowed to critique anyone that day since I hadn't put my own writing (and ego) on the line.

So, after moving to another town and joining another critique group, I dutifully took a manuscript with me, only to discover that I was expected to just listen the first time. (I didn't last long there!) **So don't assume anything.** Ask the group ahead of time for any rules they have about how the meeting is run. It will save awkwardness and hurt feelings.

Be sure you can attend the meetings. Don't join unless you can be at all the meetings (except for true emergencies). A good group member is dedicated. If you expect to give thoughtful criticism to someone's novel, then you must be there to hear it all.

Works in Progress
Secondly, the manuscripts you will be critiquing are also works in progress. If you are critiquing book manuscripts, that can be especially confusing. For example, when I joined one group, I was sent the middle chapters of several novels-in-progress. I had no idea what came before, so it was hard to critique. Was the plot building naturally? Were the characters behaving believably? I had no idea.

I would suggest, when joining a critique group, that you ask each writer for a one or two paragraph summary of what's already happened in the book so you're up to speed. Otherwise your critique can be less than helpful, and possibly irritating. For example, you may think a minor character is described in too much detail, when in fact, it was revealed earlier to be the story's villain who plays a key role. Every time something like this has to be explained to you during the meeting, it eats up valuable time.

How to Critique

Encourage as well as offer criticism. It means walking a fine line, but you must have this crucial balance if you're going to join and remain in a critique group. Encouragement is so important in a career that is, at least initially, filled with rejection. So when you join a critique group, remember that *you are part of a support group*, and some members will require more support than others.

Unless you already know everyone in the group on an intimate level, hold back from talking too much at first. Some members will want tough, "no nonsense" critiques and "skip the fluff." Others need their constructive criticism wrapped in extra layers of cotton to dull the sharp edge. Don't assume that people in the critique group will all respond to criticism the way you would. Watch and learn first!

On the flip side, when you are critiqued, don't be touchy. Defensiveness is a HUGE waste of time. Simply listen and take notes of what is said. If you don't agree with someone's critique of your work, don't spend time defending it. If it didn't work for that reader, it didn't work. That doesn't mean you have to change a word, but don't argue about it.

Do's and Don'ts

Be sure that your attitude is really one of caring, even when you don't like a particular manuscript. Point out the good spots and strengths you found first. Then give criticism so that it's constructive. Get your points across without being overly harsh or critical though. Find the balance! Be more quiet than normal the first critique session as you watch how other members handle this sensitive issue within the group.

However, you do need to learn how to express constructive criticism in a way that it can be received. Be kind in your criticism. At the same time it is important to the writer to hear everything, not just the praise. Otherwise how can they improve? Give them something to go home and work on so the critique time is productive. (Phrases like "Have you considered . . .?" and "Another way to approach the opening might be . . ." work better than flat pronouncements like "I think the ending is blah," or "I think you should do it this way.")

Critique groups are valuable, and finding a good one already "in progress" is a joy. With a few common sense tips and attitudes, you'll slip in without making a ripple (instead of creating tidal waves). In a few short weeks, it'll be as if you'd always belonged.

Mentors or Tormentors?

I have had two experiences with mentoring, both very positive. I was on the receiving end at a week-long writers' conference, and my mentor was a much published author in a field I wanted to enter. She was open and encouraging and offered excellent constructive criticism.

I have also had the privilege of mentoring another writer through a mentorship program that lasted a year. I was on the giving end this time, and besides making a new friend, I think I was helpful to this newer writer.

Black and White
Famous writers, both present and past, talk fondly of mentors who supported them through the rough early years of writing. Books are lovingly dedicated to mentors who believed in these writers when the rest of the world didn't.

But before you snatch up the first willing mentor you find, be aware that not all mentors are created equal. The mentor you pair up with may actually be a tormentor in disguise. While attempting to "help" you, a tormentor inflicts torture, pain, confusion, and vexation. Just what you need, right? No!

Despite the many "happily ever after" stories you hear, there are unfortunately also destructive outcomes from mentoring relationships. Promising young authors turn their backs on writing forever because their "mentor" pronounced their stories naive, lacking or boring. "You'll never be a writer!" is the message given, intentionally or not, by these critical and egotistical professional writers. You may not know you've found a tormentor instead of a mentor until you're a few weeks into the relationship. But look for the danger signs, and if you see them, *terminate this relationship.*

> In these tough publishing days, could you benefit from finding a true mentor? Quite possibly, but first, let's define the term. A mentor is not a critique partner, although some mentors do critique as well. A mentor is primarily a trusted counselor, advisor, guide, tutor, or coach. It's someone who is further along in her writing career—sometimes much further—who is willing to take you under her wing and show you the ropes and encourage you through the rough periods. A mentor is worth her weight in ink cartridges.

Healthy Mentor Qualities

As with any relationship, there are healthy (and unhealthy) mentor/mentee pairings. If you know that you have a propensity to let people abuse or walk all over you, if you lack healthy boundaries and can't protect your self-esteem, be especially careful when choosing a mentor. While an oppressive friend or relative can drain your creativity, an oppressive writing mentor can derail your dreams and kill your faith in your writing ability. A lengthy relationship with a writing tormentor can leave long-term (even permanent) damage.

So how do you recognize a healthy mentor? She needs the same qualities as a well balanced parent. You don't want a permissive mentor, who (like a permissive parent) heaps on the praise and lets you do and think whatever you please, offering no insights or course corrections. This kind of mentor is no help in the real writing world.

On the other extreme, you don't want an authoritarian mentor either. Like an overbearing parent, this type of mentor finds fault easily, overlooks your strengths, and bludgeons you with your shortcomings. This type of mentor may mean well, but the criticism is relentless and your self-esteem plummets.

Helpful Signs

You want a balanced mentor to help guide and encourage you along the writing path. This type of trainer or coach uses encouragement plus accountability to help you grow. The encouragement is positive, but so is the accountability. In fact, good mentors are balanced and function much like good teachers. He will "inspire but not dictate, praise without making someone overconfident, and critique without humiliating or discouraging," according to Elizabeth Berg in *Escaping into the Open.*

If you find that meetings with your mentor leave you feeling "less than" about your writing or yourself, if you feel discouraged instead of bolstered, then it's possible that your mentor is (not necessarily on purpose) a tormentor. If so, ease out of the relationship and find another mentor.

High Expectations

We are happiest in relationships where our expectations are realistic and not based on fantasy. What kind of expectations of yourself should you have in this relationship? First, try to be open-minded to your mentor's suggestions. You have presumably chosen a mentor who knows more of the ropes than you do about the writing life, so at least consider her ideas for such things as:

- juggling writing and parenting
- how to be a savvy marketer
- how to discover your passions
- how to dig deeper into characters
- how to write more consistently

Don't be too quick to trot out your excuses of why her suggestions won't work in your special situation.

Second, what are your expectations of your mentor? Discuss these expectations openly when first introduced. Your expectations may be unrealistic.

- Your mentor is there to encourage you, not to spend more time on your writing than you do.
- Do not expect your mentor to use her publishing contacts to help you get published.
- Your mentor is not "on call" night or day to hold your hand.
- Do not expect her to stay hours beyond your meeting time to discuss your work or other concerns with you.

She *might* do some of those things, but you should not expect her to.

Choosing a Mentor

If you are active in the writing field, you will meet other writers at conferences, book discussion groups, bookstore events, book signings, and writing workshops. Out of all the more experienced writers you meet, how do you spot a good candidate to approach for a mentor relationship? To think of names of writers you might contact, consider the following things:

1) Whom in your field do you respect, and what qualities in them do you admire?
2) What person/people do you call upon when you either need help or want to celebrate? This is the type of helpful (not critical) personality you want in a mentor.
3) What habits do they have that would help you? Are they organized, creative, or outspoken where you're disorganized, obscure or shy?
4) What are they doing that you would like to be doing yourself? What is happening in their writing life that you would love to see happening in yours?

Never Too Old!

One last thing: never assume because you're published or have been in the writing field a long time that you can't benefit from having a mentor, even if it's only for three to six months. We all get derailed from time to time and need help getting back on track. We all go through personal and professional life changes and can use bolstering and redirection during the down times.

And if, by chance, your writing life is everything you ever dreamed of, how about mentoring another struggling writer who could benefit from your encouragement? Look around you. It won't take long to find one!

(NOTE: People are very busy, so if your first inquiry to a potential mentor gets turned down, try not to feel rejected. It isn't personal. I know—I've had to turn people down myself. Also, if you have the money, consider hiring a writing coach or taking an online mentoring course.)

Writing Through Physical Pain

When my kids were toddlers and in grade school, my jaw was wired shut for eleven weeks after two surgeries. I'd had some health problems over the years, but being wired shut topped them all. I couldn't talk to my four small children or even call a friend. (And this was before the Internet, email and chat rooms.) I was thoroughly cut off.

I was dying to talk, but couldn't. So I hurried to my computer where my characters "talked" onscreen to each other. Dialogue flew back and forth, and (rather surprisingly) this mental conversation went a long ways toward satisfying me. Writing a middle-grade novel usually took me five or six months. This time, being stuck at home and unable to talk, it took me two months to write *Danger at Hanging Rock*, turning this post-surgical problem into salable writing.

A Real Pain

Writing *about* pain and writing *through* pain is possible. Not FUN, but possible. Health problems crop up routinely. They range from short-term problems (like your son's broken leg), to things needing constant close attention (like diabetes or arthritis). The most serious problems (terminal illness or a death in the family) affect us all, sooner or later.

However, instead of quitting, we can also transform these experiences into publishable writing, whether it's a simple case of the flu or a stay in the hospital. It's tempting with short-term health problems to abandon our writing "until things settle down." If at all possible, don't do that.

Instead, stand back, rethink, and keep going. For example, I finished a mystery called *Cast a Single Shadow* during my four-year-old daughter's hospital stay. I couldn't sleep, so to meet my deadline, I borrowed a nurse's clipboard and wrote while my daughter and the rest of the hospital slept.

Chronic Pain: Another Story

I've had TMJ, facial nerve damage from several surgeries, and arthritis in my jaw joints for thirty years. I've also had five neck surgeries to deal with a chronic pain condition. The two main challenges for writers and artists with chronic pain are (1) finding the energy to write, and (2) fighting depression.

Writing, as you know, demands a high level of energy, and people fighting chronic pain may use 30-50% of their daily energy just fighting their pain. If chronic pain threatens to stop you from writing, try these things:

Accept pain as a fact in your life. Don't compare your life with anyone else's or brood about "how life should be." It won't help. Books like Judy Gann's excellent title *The God of All Comfort: Devotions of Hope for Those Who Chronically Suffer* will help and encourage you. You'll realize that many others deal with chronic pain—and overcome it. You can too.

Fight the depression. If possible, try writing about the positive aspects of your situation. ("Life's Simple Pleasures" was an article written by a migraine sufferer about learning to appreciate what most people take for granted, like a night's sleep, a picnic with the family, or planting tulips.) Any type of writing you enjoy is helpful in fighting depression because it tends to distract you from your pain (like when you forget your headache during an exciting movie).

Find the energy. Create mini-goals (for example, writing just fifteen minutes at a time). Divide each writing task into very thin, achievable slices. Assure yourself that you only have to complete one mini-goal or slice, then stop if you need to. Pace your activities, even on the days you feel better than usual. Pushing yourself on your good days only increases chronic pain in the long run.

Terminal Illness

Terminal illness and a death in the family tax your creativity the most. The shock, numbness, and months of extended grief can derail even the most dedicated writers. However, even in these cases, certain strategies can keep you going.

Why would you even *want* to keep writing during such a stressful time? The point of it is so that you still have a career when the weeks or months have passed. You won't have to start over at Square One. Yes, you take the necessary time to grieve or deal with things. However, if you put your writing "on hold" until things are "back to normal," you may find it too difficult to get started again later.

Keeping that in mind, some tips for writing during a really rough patch might include:

Journal your feelings. Journal in hospitals, waiting rooms, and cafeterias. Your deepest heart-felt thoughts will provide excellent material for later. They may become fillers, daily devotions or even greeting card verses for people in similar circumstances.

Encourage and coax, but *don't push yourself to write.* Burnout occurs when the demands we put on ourselves outweigh our energy supply. Some days you just won't be able to put pen to paper.

Again, write about your experiences. It can be the best healer of all. To deal with the pain after my dad died twenty-eight years ago, I wrote *The Rose Beyond the Wall*, a middle-grade novel about a grandmother with terminal cancer. It was a book written from the heart. Despite its subject, it's a hopeful book for children, and it sold well in hardcover and paperback. Think about doing the same thing with your experiences.

Remember that "this too shall pass," and when it does, you'll be in a position to share with others what you've learned. That's a writer's satisfaction that money can't buy.

Mindful? Or Multi-Tasker?

If you're a writer and a parent (or a writer, parent and have a day job), you already multi-task. Many of you, to accomplish all that needs to be done in a day, multi-*multi*-task. Just this week, in a car next to me at a stop light, was a mom putting on her make-up, talking on her cell phone, and feeding her child a snack. When the light turned green, I couldn't watch. How did she also *drive*?

Most of us learned to multi-task out of necessity. It's a survival skill. We had huge to-do lists (either written down or swimming in our brain) that needed to be tackled. With a fixed number of hours in the day, we learned to do two or three things at once. It's a great skill to have! However, even the time management experts admit that we over-do it sometimes.

The Downside of Multi-Tasking

I certainly survived the young mom/writer/teacher years by multi-tasking. I would never have found time to write if I hadn't. And yes, it makes perfect sense to multi-task some things, especially non-think types of activities. You can fold clothes while listening to the news, or read a magazine while you're on hold to make an appointment.

However, things suffer when you combine two or more activities that both require your brain to be engaged. Listening to your child tell about her school day while you're proofing your manuscript short-changes both activities. Long-term multi-tasking jobs (like air traffic controllers, managers of emergency rooms, and working single parents) eventually affect the brain and can lead to burn-out (or even breakdowns).

Studies show that long-term multi-tasking actually *lowers your effectiveness, generates mistakes, and contributes to a host of health problems.* And it becomes very difficult—even when you have time—to slow down, think about one idea, write about it, and stick with the project for any length of time.

Mindfulness: The Alternative

Is there honestly an alternative to the chicken-with-her-head-cut-off frenzied multi-tasking that many of us use to get through our days? Yes, there is, although it may sound impossible. It's called "mindfulness." It's concentrating on one activity at a time. It reduces stress and time pressure and that pervasive agitated feeling.

I don't believe it's an either/or proposition. I think a healthy writer needs to be able to BOTH multi-task and be mindful. Knowing *when* to be mindful and *when* to multi-task is the key. Often it's something you must learn by trial and error.

> When you try to settle down to write, are you plagued by time pressure, distractions, interruptions, conflicts with your spouse or kids, or other agitating problems? Believe it or not, you can cure each of these writing problems with "mindfulness."

On my computer is a clipping from an article published by The Benson Henry Institute for Mind Body Medicine. The quote says:

> *"Mindfulness is . . . the practice of learning to pay attention to what is happening to you from moment to moment. To be mindful, you must slow down, do one activity at a time and bring your full awareness to both the activity at hand and to your inner experience of it. Mindfulness provides a potentially powerful antidote to the common causes of daily stress, such as time pressure, distraction, agitation and interpersonal conflicts."*

Basically, mindfulness is the exact opposite of multi-tasking, the skill most of us use to survive and are secretly (or not so secretly) proud of. We women especially are smug about our ability to juggle ten balls in the air at one time while our male counterparts move methodically from one mental box to the next, and never the boxes do overlap. I hate to admit it, but as far as writing goes, men have the edge in being able to focus, simply by how their brains are wired.

Focused vs. Scattered

Mindfulness is really another word for *focus*, the ability to place your mental energies in one place, not scattered to the four winds. Mindfulness is like using a magnifying glass to focus a sunbeam onto the pavement. Scattered, the sunlight is pleasantly warm. Focused? You can fry an egg.

My "to do" list grew last week while I dealt with computer problems, did a paid critique, babysat grandchildren, and wrote a book review (after reading the book). So when I made out my work schedule this week, it was a bit overwhelming with "left-over" tasks from last week. But today I read and re-read that quote about mindfulness, then decided to concentrate on one item at a time.

I focused, like a horse wearing blinders, and it worked. Yes, during the first half hour, I had to continually bring my mind back to the task. But after that, my multi-tasking brain got the hint and settled down. A surprising amount of work got done—and without headaches and agitation.

Mindfulness. Try it. You might like it!

Perfectionist Writers

I woke up at 2 a.m. and couldn't go back to sleep. I wasn't sick, and I was still sleepy, but that relentless voice in my head wouldn't shut up. It reminded me of the long "should do" list waiting in my office that day.

I dragged myself out of bed, hoping to get a jump on the day and have a fighting chance of getting everything done. Before I headed down the hall to my office, I made some hot chocolate and read a magazine article. I had to laugh—the article could have been written just for me. Maybe for you too?

All Wound Up

It was about the pressure of perfectionism (which shows up in more ways than I thought). In "Permission to Exhale," Joan C. Webb, author of *The Relief of Imperfection*, talked about the pressures we face as women. (I'm sure men face their own set of impossible expectations these days too.) I suspect the following attitude creeps into your writing. I know it deeply affects mine.

She wrote:

> *"The pressure is everywhere. Books, magazines, commercials, reality shows, Internet pop-ups, stores, fitness centers, and even churches present methods and habits we can and should adopt so we can: look younger and trimmer; be healthier and more energetic; work faster and better at home or in the office; be more successful; make extra money; maintain consistently satisfying relationships; obtain more education; improve our cooking, time management, home décor, and parenting skills; build a bigger, better, and more*

organized house; be a more loving mate; and enjoy more leisure time—all while avoiding overload, reducing anxiety and stress, growing personally and spiritually, and giving generously to the hungry and hurting . . . and doing it all with greater joy, peace, and passion."

Doesn't that statement leave you *exhausted*? It's funny—but oh! So true!

Frantically Treading Water

Over the years, I've done a good job of single-handedly keeping the self-help book industry afloat. I've bought dozens of books on every one of those subjects except home décor, and my comfortable (but un-fancy home) testifies to that. I've done the same self-help-for-perfectionists routine in my writing life, and the six book shelves in my home office prove it. Why is that?

As the author mentions later, all advertising makes two statements. First, "you're deficient." And second, "if you buy this, it will fix that." The self-help industry stays in business that way. Don't get me wrong—I've been helped enormously in ALL those self-help categories by some books I've read, and I'm grateful for the authors who shared their experiences, secrets and practical tips with me. But I want to talk about the subtle—but very real—pressure the advice can put on us to then perform perfectly, both as people and as writers.

I'm tired of the relentless messages that tell me I'm deficient as a writer. "You don't market enough—buy this book and you can fix that!" "You're not inspired enough—hire me as your coach and fix that!" "You're not organized enough—listen to my paid webinar and fix that!" Some of the services and books I've bought online *have* been fabulous, and I've blogged about many of them, and will continue to do so when I find ones that are especially helpful to me. I'm just talking here about the *flood* of emails trying to make me feel flawed in my career so I will buy something to fix it.

Bombarded

I don't know about you, but over the years I've subscribed to a couple dozen free e-newsletters. Many are terrific, although I have less and less time to read them. But frequently I unsubscribe because of the annoying amount of "other" email that comes along with it: advertising for seminars and ebooks and webinars and services I don't want. I don't like the pressure it creates.

Calgon, Take Me Away!

So what's the solution for perfectionist writers? One more book? One more seminar or webinar? Or might it be simpler than that?

It may well be something I read in *Art & Fear: Observations on the Perils (and Rewards) of Artmaking* by David Bayles and Ted Orland. I found it very encouraging. Maybe you will too. It was about being a perfectionist—and how to overcome the pressure it generates in all artists, including writers. Read about this experiment:

> *The ceramics teacher announced on opening day that he was dividing the class into two groups. All those on the left side of the studio, he said, would be graded solely on the quantity of work they produced, all those on the right solely on its quality. His procedure was simple: on the final day of class, he would bring in his bathroom scales and weigh the work of the "quantity" group: fifty pounds of pots rated an "A", forty pounds a "B", and so on. Those being graded on "quality", however, needed to produce only one pot—albeit a perfect one—to get an "A". Well, came grading time and a curious fact emerged: the works of highest quality were all produced by the group being graded for quantity. It seems that while the "quantity" group was busily churning out piles of work— and learning from their mistakes—the "quality" group had sat theorizing about perfection, and in the end had little more to show for their efforts than grandiose theories and a pile of dead clay.*

Quality from Quantity

Isn't that a fascinating experiment? It's been proven that we get better by writing more, like a piano player gets better by practicing more. But what struck me is how much more FUN the first group must have had (while at the same time producing superior pots). They were just trying to create a lot of pots. They were, therefore, putting in a lot of practice—but with no emphasis on perfection.

Could I use the results of this experiment to revamp my own writing that was often stalled by the perfectionist demon?

I decided to try an experiment of my own. Most days I more closely resemble a pot maker from Group B: stewing, not writing, being unhappy with results when I finally *do* write, scrapping them, judging, blocking, and finally quitting for the day.

For one day, I decided to be a Group A pot-making writer—and just relax. I stayed off the Internet till noon and just wrote—a lot. My only goal was to produce a lot of pages. I wrote for three hours, and I had fun! From what I can tell, the finished pages aren't half bad either—and I produced more than three times my usual daily quantity.

I think I'm onto something here!

Misplaced Dreams

In an email newsletter, *Living Your Dreams—The Internet Newsletter of the Center for Balanced Living*, a paragraph by author Stacy Mayo leaped out at me. Why? Because (almost verbatim) they were the words I'd been asking myself all weekend about a project that has limped along for over a year. Here's what jolted me:

> *"No matter how successful you are, likelihood is there is some idea you are dabbling with. What is in the way of you committing to this idea? To really going for it? To playing it out to see what is possible? To see what kind of an impact you can have if you just get out of your own way? I encourage you to make a decision one way or another but to quit dabbling. Either decide to go for this idea in a way that is exciting and fun for you or let it go."*

She's Reading My Mail!

That's the decision I needed to make. Either go for it in a committed way—or let it go.

Over a year ago, I had an idea for an ambitious writing project, one that would require more time, some serious study, more research than I was used to, and lots of work. I ran the idea past an agent and my critique group, and they all thought it was a great idea. I was glad—I'd wanted to stretch myself as a writer for a number of years. This project was my chance.

I started out like a house on fire, but over the last year or so, the fire has fizzled. Hardly a spark anymore—even though I still really like the idea and the first hundred pages I've written. One thing after another came up, and weeks passed while I was (legitimately) "too busy" to write. And yet . . . the idea nags at me, and I actually *loooong* to get the idea down on paper.

So what's the problem? I had no idea. I've never had this problem before, not in thirty years of writing and publishing forty-two books. But I think I found the answer recently when flipping through the course notes from Margie Lawson's "Defeat Self-Defeating Behaviors" class. What caught my eye was under the heading of "Failure to Produce."

> *"Sometimes writers keep themselves too busy with life distractions so they have excuses to not progress with their book. Are these legitimate? Or, are they protecting themselves from failing? If they never finish writing the book, they'll never have to face the fear of rejection. What if I do my best and I still fail . . ."*

Whammy!
There it was! I'd seen it in my students for years and encouraged procrastinating writer friends past such obstacles. But I couldn't see it in myself! However, these words rang true. This ambitious project I had tackled had me scared. I feared that I was over-reaching my writing skills and didn't want to face possible failure. After all, if you don't finish your book, you can't get rejected.

Fear of Failure? Me?
I'm hopeful—I know I'm on the right track. It's time to work on combating this common writing fear—and then get to work. I'm eager to get back to that project and move ahead to completion.

Writing Habits That Help You

Change: Making It Stick

Have you ever had a wake-up call that was loud enough to make you change your lifestyle? Maybe you developed a stress-related disease or had a heart attack. Have you ever procrastinated about changing (maybe for years) and then suddenly been able to make that change—and make it stick?

I have—so that proves that I have the ability. I bet you do too. So why can't we make permanent changes with our writing? And marketing? Instead, I find myself continually making excuses for not getting the work done, excuses like:

- "My back and neck hurt."
- "I don't have anything worthwhile to say."
- "I can't write when I'm emotionally upset."
- "This is so boring."

Why do I allow those excuses to end in relapse? What is it that motivates us to make a *permanent* lifestyle change? And how can we apply that knowledge to our writing?

Big Scares
Sometimes the motivator/wake-up call is a big scare of some kind. I have a friend who is now motivated to lose 140 pounds because his last complication—a broken blood vessel in the brain—was painful enough to get his attention.

Last year, I got my own wake-up call. A check-up revealed a high cholesterol reading, and I was told I had three months to get it down with diet, or I'd have to take drugs. Drugs and I don't mix well *at all*, and that was enough to motivate me to eat a *very* low fat diet (only cheating once in three months) and to exercise daily.

Both my friend and I have known for years that we needed to make changes. And we'd both tried—and failed—and tried—and quit. (*Many* times.) And yet, when faced with dire consequences, we were able to do what needed to be done—and make the necessary once-and-for-all lifestyle change.

Slave Drivers

Sometimes the motivator for a lifestyle change is some kind of slave driver. I remember working in an office for seven months where I actually had three bosses. I hated that boring job. My neck and back hurt then too. But I was at my desk by 8:30 daily, I never took longer than my allotted 15-minute break, and I didn't take personal calls or play on the Internet when I was supposed to be working. Why not? I needed to keep my job—and at least one of the bosses was always looking over my shoulder.

Or what about all those boring high school and college classes? For me, it was the world history and economics classes that put me to sleep. Or tried to. However, bored as I was, I found a way to stay awake and sit in my chair until the 55 minutes were over. How? Alphabetically I always ended up sitting near the front of the class, under someone's piercing eye. They pounced on you with questions if they suspected you were sleeping with your eyes open.

I used all the tricks I could muster to stay alert. Why? I wanted the grade. It didn't matter if my stomach hurt or I'd had a big fight with my boyfriend or I was bored to tears. I showed up for class—and I did the work.

Can't Do It—or Won't?

As I thought about the above scenarios, I realized that it was a blatant lie to tell myself I couldn't write for longer periods of time. I've had to work for long periods before. It was a lie to tell myself that I couldn't sit still that long, that I needed constant breaks and rewards and bribes to keep writing. I had never had a boss or a teacher dangle carrots before me, whispering, "You can do it! You can stick it out! Just ten more minutes and you'll be done!"

Heavens, no. It hadn't been necessary then. I had to admit that it wasn't necessary now.

What's the Answer?

If we want to make a lifestyle writing change, one where we write daily for longer periods of time without all the procrastination, what can we use as a similar motivator? What can substitute for the boss watching from his desk? What is a *wake-up call for writing* equivalent to a health scare?

What incentive can we use to smack ourselves up the side of the head so we stop this incessant messing around, *once and for all*, and get to work daily? How can we make that permanent lifestyle writing change?

Sometimes a desperate need for income will do it. When I was the fulltime writer who was also the sole breadwinner for my family, the slave driver was built in automatically. Work daily and work hard, or your family won't eat or have a place to live. Open and shut case. No matter how I felt, I got to work the minute the school bus picked up my kids.

That isn't the case anymore. My kids are grown, and my income only contributes to the household. No one will starve if I stop writing. So I'm looking for something to motivate me to stop the constant waffling between my disciplined writing days and my procrastination days (which effectively cancel out those disciplined days).

Tired of the Drama

> All this writing angst, year after year, is starting to strike me as rather . . . well . . . *silly*. Drama queen kind of stuff. I wonder, in the end, if the lifestyle change will involve nothing more than telling myself to just "stop it!"

Recently when I sat down at my writing desk and looked at my blank writing paper, I closed my eyes and pictured my boring econ class, then my boring secretarial job, and how many hours I'd forced myself to work in both cases. Then I looked at my story—something I'm excited about and enjoy working on (once I get into it).

Just for that day, I tried telling myself *"I can"* statements. I said,

"I can sit here for an hour without a break," and "I can write for two hours this morning," and "I can focus regardless of my physical health," and "I've done lots harder things than *this* before!" and a few other true statements, based on past experiences.

The Proof

And guess what? I wrote for two hours, with a short break in the middle, before turning to the blog and other marketing and critiquing I needed to do that day. I wrote about 2,650 new words, and it felt wonderfully productive.

I'm going to choose to do that each day. And the day after that. And the day after that. Eventually I'll have that lifestyle change.

"Not To-Do" List

I once had an apartment with one large hall closet. At first it was roomy and organized. Over the two years I lived there, it grew more and more crowded and chaotic as I stuffed more and more junk into it. One day, I realized I couldn't jam one more thing in there and still close the door. Something was going to have to come OUT before more would go IN.

Time Is Like a Closet

One year I took some online classes plus set up a self-study program to grow in my writing craft. It would require around four hours per day to do everything I wanted to do. Given the fact that I NEVER had four free hours in a day, where was that time going to come from?

One thing I love to do on January 1 is change calendars: wall calendars in kitchen and office, desk calendars (daily and monthly) in my office, and pocket calendars for my purse. The squares of the New Year calendar pages are virtually pristine and pure. An occasional appointment already filled a square or two, but that's all.

The calendars I pitch have perhaps only one or two clean white squares per month with nothing scheduled. Just looking at them makes me feel tired. I know from experience, though, that the clean calendars will soon look just as jam-packed as the old calendars if I don't take steps NOW to prevent it.

But *how*?

Create a "NOT To-Do" List

To make time for some new things I wanted to do, I had to look at the calendar and find the time wasters. Some events are important to me and will stay on my new schedule: our weekly potluck supper with my grown kids and grandkids, teaching Sunday school at the Air Force base to basic trainees, my every-other-week critique group, leading DivorceCare at church, and blogging three times a week. These activities feed my goals of a strong extended family, volunteer service, and growth as a writer.

However, I noticed a LOT of stuff on my calendar that could *easily* go. (Well, easily in the sense that I wouldn't miss it. *Difficult* in the sense that it would mean saying "no" more often—and people pleasers like me hate that.)

My Personal "Not To-Do" List

I know the Internet eats up a lot of time for me. This year I've decided to stay offline until noon by adding the blog the night before so it posts automatically in the morning without me being online. Before I go to bed at night, I remove the laptop (which has the Internet connection) from my office altogether. It's easier to deal with the temptation this way. Out of sight, out of mind! Reading other people's blogs, posting on Twitter and Facebook, and answering email can wait till later in the day.

No more "come and buy something" parties. I don't like parties selling jewelry, home interior decorations, clothing, pots and pans, etc. I am also going to limit how many invitations I accept to showers. At my age, every woman is having grandkids and giving baby showers for friends having new grandkids. I rarely know their children or grandchildren. The shower only appears to take two hours, but by the time you've bought and wrapped a gift, gotten yourself ready, and driven to and from in heavy city traffic, it kills about eight hours. A gift card in the mail would be fine most of the time. (Not sure I'll ever get up the guts to RSVP with, "Hey, I've never even met your kid, and I barely even know you, so I won't be coming or sending a gift.") Sounds very Scroogey, I know. But ooooh, so tempting.

I will no longer clean the house before the every-other-month visit by the Orkin bug man.

I won't attend more than one social function per weekend, no matter how much I love the people. Social functions wear me out, keep me up too late to get a good night's sleep, and because talking aggravates my TMJ, it results in headaches. I was astounded how many things were on the calendar that I didn't enjoy. (Example: both my husband and I hate football, so why are we going to Super Bowl parties every year?)

I will stop scheduling necessary doctor and dentist appointments in the middle of my work day.

This is just a beginning, but I think you get the idea.

Your Assignment

Your task, if you decide to accept it, is to look at your old calendar and make a list of things you no longer want to do. Prune away the events, committees, and jobs that have become time wasters keeping you from fulfilling your own higher priority goals and commitments.

> Keep the list near your phone. Practice saying, "Thank you for asking me (or inviting me), but I'm afraid I will have to say NO at this time." End of discussion.
>
> You can do it! I can do it! Having a "NOT To-Do" list is the only way we'll be able to have a writer's "To-Do" list that is effective.

Counting the Cost

Few things in life worth having are free. They may not cost you money, but they will cost you in time and effort.

According to leadership expert John Maxwell, "People embark on a new career path with energy and enthusiasm, only to fizzle out when they realize how much effort is involved." This usually happens because they didn't count the cost first. They didn't figure out what it would take for them to be successful. They didn't realize there would be a price to pay.

This doesn't need to happen to you. To make it through the long haul, ask yourself: what does it cost to have a successful writing career? What price must I be willing to pay? Based on thirty years of experience, I'd include the following:

Hard work: Suppose you desire the career of some well-known writer. Are you willing to make the effort she made to get there? This includes doing things you don't enjoy (like marketing), writing while others sleep or play, and keeping day jobs until your writing income increases. According to *On Writing*'s best-selling author Stephen King, "Talent is cheaper than table salt. What separates the talented individual from the successful one is a lot of hard work."

Learning: Achieving your writing and illustrating dreams will require learning new skills. It may involve reading books and attending workshops. Depending on how and where you choose to learn, this will cost time, money, and energy. There are free sources: library books and writing websites packed with excellent articles. You can also learn through college courses, home study courses, online writing courses, local and national Society of Children's Book Writers and Illustrators events, and writers' conferences. (Check the *Shaw Guides* at www.shawguides.com for an extensive list of conferences and workshops.)

Discipline and stamina: It takes daily focus to pursue your goal without getting sidetracked or giving up. You need to make right choices consistently and usually daily. Discipline may be an acquired taste, depending on your personality, but without it, your dreams will remain just that: *dreams*. Stamina is slightly different. It means having the discipline to keep going despite setbacks, bad writing days, rejections, and bad reviews.

Healthy lifestyle: Writing—unless it's a hobby that you dabble at— is hard physical work. Tired minds and bodies don't create well. Overfed and under-exercised bodies give out too soon. Trade late night TV for extra sleep. Eliminate diets heavy in fat and sugar in favor of fresh fruits and vegetables. Do daily aerobics. Get your body in shape to support your dream. Don't think you can skip this tip! As the years go by, it will get MORE important, not less so.

Setting boundaries: Learn to say no. Practice saying "I'm not available that day," and "I already have plans that evening," and "no, I'm so sorry, but I can't." You may have to set boundaries with friends, bosses, spouses, in-laws, or children—anyone who doesn't want to allow you time to write.

Sacrifice: To find time to pursue your dreams and still keep your important relationships flourishing, you'll need to sacrifice something of your own as well as setting a few boundaries. It may mean giving up lunches with friends, raising prize-winning roses, or listening to talk radio. Then fill those "found" hours with reading professional magazines and recently published children's books—and WRITING.

Will You Pay the Price?

Often I hear from my students that they are just too busy (with volunteer activities, family obligations, hobbies, vacations, and pets) to be able to focus on writing. That's okay. But they need to understand that you can't have it all and do it all—and still be a successful writer.

The price you may have to pay in order to keep your day job and take care of your family relationships is pursuing this one single activity (writing) while putting everything else on hold for a while. If you want big results, and you're already juggling a lot of responsibilities, the price tag will be large too.

Sacrifices

Part of paying the price is the willingness to do whatever it takes to get the job done. Intend to get it done no matter how long it takes, no matter what comes up. "It's a done deal. You are responsible for the results you intend. No excuses," says Jack Canfield (co-creator of the *Chicken Soup for the Soul* books) in *The Success Principles*.

Is the price ever too high to pay? Yes, it might be if you insist on an impossible timetable to achieve success. It's not worth sacrificing your health or truly neglecting your family. *But it doesn't have to be all or nothing.* You don't have to choose between quitting your day job to write fulltime and giving up your writing dreams altogether. Instead, bite off what you can chew—even if it's only "write daily on my lunch break at work"—and then chew it consistently. You'd be amazed how much you can accomplish in one solid uninterrupted writing hour per day.

Making the Crucial Decision

Are you willing to pay the price? To find out:

1) Read about writers, talk to published writers, and find out the true cost of their writing success.
2) Then decide if you're willing to pay that price.

Don't be impulsive or let your enthusiasm make your decision for you. Take plenty of time to really think. When you're ready, make a quality, 100%, no-turning-back decision about the price you're willing to pay. Write these things down, date the paper, and sign it. *You've just made the most important decision of your writing career.*

Focus: The Power of Scheduling

"I don't care how much power, brilliance, or energy you have, if you don't harness it and FOCUS it on a specific target, and hold it there, you're never going to accomplish as much as your ability warrants."

— Zig Ziglar, author and motivational speaker

There are two kinds of focus for writers to consider. First is the type that has to do with marketing yourself and your work. You can be a generalist or a focused writer. Generalists take on all sorts of assignments—short stories, web writing, work-for-hire test passage writing, blogging for money, ghost writing books, etc. And there's nothing wrong with any type of writing.

The trouble is that generalists are never recognized as experts in anything. And it's the experts who are paid big bucks for their expertise. So take some time to decide if you want to be a generalist or if you want to focus on particular topics or genres. Where do you want to concentrate your writing energies?

Focal Point
The second kind of focus has to do with taking the necessary steps to achieve the goals we've set for ourselves. If you don't focus, you can end up trying to juggle too many balls in the air. Most of us try to do too many things at once, flitting from one thing to another with the attention span of a four-year-old. We get distracted by all we need to do, so we change direction every five minutes.

> We don't use our time, resources, or skills optimally. We work very hard, but not very smart. At the end of most days, we haven't accomplished much. "We are emotional and reactive, rather than methodical and strategic," says one motivational speaker. We don't **focus**. We need single-minded, unwavering determination and focus, not occasional bursts of enthusiasm.

So how can we achieve this second kind of focus to make the best use of the time we have? It's called *scheduling*.

A Simple Solution

Many times I've felt overwhelmed when looking at the various writing projects waiting on my desk. Given a choice, I'm a one-project-at-a-time gal. I'd prefer not to work on a second project until the first one is complete, polished, and submitted.

However, more and more in recent years, I find myself in the middle of several projects at once: a nonfiction teen book requested by an editor, a fiction series proposal which needs sample chapters written, a serious middle grade novel that needs revision, and a lot of marketing ideas for my websites. I get "Mexican jumping bean mind" and can't seem to stick with any project, but bounce from one thing to another.

Not only is that very frustrating, it doesn't produce much work by the end of the day.

What's the Solution?

I believe the "Morning Nudge" by Suzanne Lieurance (from the *Working Writer's Coach* blog) has the solution. When I read it, I knew I'd hit pay dirt.

> *People always ask me why I'm not stressed out over all the things I have to do every day. My answer is simple. I schedule everything. Once something is on my schedule, I don't think about it anymore until the scheduled time for it. That way, I'm able to relax and focus on just one thing at a time. I also avoid guilty feelings when I'm enjoying myself because I schedule leisure activities into each day as well as work. Scheduling is very powerful. Try it!*

So that's what I did. I sorted notebooks and papers into project piles. Then I tackled one pile at a time, in order of priorities. (A requested book manuscript always takes priority with me.) With calendar and daily planner in hand, I mapped out deadlines, then broke all the projects down into very manageable pieces.

Nuts and Bolts of Scheduling

I already knew that I could work in 90-minute blocks at the computer before getting neck pain and headaches. So while making the schedule, I penciled in breaks after each 90-minute working segment. For me, it has to be get-away-from-the-computer time, both to rest my eyes and to exercise my back and neck. (For example: weed a flower bed, water plants, walk, sit in the porch swing, load the dishwasher, watch ten minutes of a favorite movie, listen to ten minutes of a book on tape, etc.)

I came back refreshed, and with my brain ready to switch gears and focus on the next project. Part of the break time was spent thinking about the next project and mentally shifting gears.

Scheduling is both powerful and productive. I like being able to focus on one thing at a time, knowing the other projects will get their turn in due time. Slowly but surely, each project will be completed. And it's amazing how much our concentration improves when we know a reward is coming soon!

Getting the Writing Done

Slow and steady still wins the race. Even the writing race.

In an excellent interview (on the *Cynsations* blog) author Nancy Garden was asked: Over the past decade, what are the most important lessons you've learned about your craft, the writing/ artistic life, and/or publishing, and why? In part, Nancy said:

> *"I think the most important lesson I've learned about my craft—or at least about myself as a writer—over the past decade is to slow down! By that I don't necessarily mean to write less, and I certainly don't mean to take more time off (what's that?), but what I do mean is to be sure to give each new book or story all the time it needs before sending it off to one's editor or one's agent. Working on more than one book at the same time used to work for me, especially when each project was at a different stage of development or when each was different from its companions—different age levels, for example, different genres, etc. But recently, I found myself working on two or three things which were at roughly the same stage of development at more or less the same time— and that led to my impatiently releasing some before they were really ready."*

I couldn't agree more with her statements. In the last few years, I've thought a lot about where the pressure to hurry the writing comes from. In *In Praise of Slowness: Challenging the Cult of Speed*, Carl Honore says a lot more about this subject, and it's worth reading the entire book. In his chapter "Work: The Benefits of Working Less Hard," Honore talks about how technology today has allowed work to seep into every corner of our lives.

Nowhere to Hide

There is nowhere to hide from email, texts, Tweets, faxes and phone calls. Everyone is potentially on duty all the time—and often expected to be. Working from home can easily slip into working all the time. And writers are no longer exempt.

With the fairly recent emphasis on writers needing "platforms" in order to sell their books, writers feel pressured to have websites, blogs, blog tours, newsletters, book trailers, TV and radio interviews, and more. The slower methods when I started writing (typing on an old college typewriter in a tiny closet to get away from the kids) were quiet and peaceful and slower. It was a big part of the charm of the writing life to me.

But now, thanks to "hurry" pressure, even writers are caught in a time squeeze. As Honore says, "Even the simple things—taking the kids to school, eating supper, chatting with friends—become a race against the clock." Life wasn't this way when I began writing—and I was juggling four very young children underfoot and a farm and huge vegetable gardens and lots of church work. I was plenty busy!

But there was no Internet, no email, no Facebook and Twitter, no blogs, no pressure to turn out books as fast as you could type them. Your only real job was to *write* the book. If you had two hours of writing time, you wrote two hours. (Some days now, I'm lucky to write thirty minutes because the marketing jobs take a lot of time.) You could do school visits and autograph parties if you wanted to, but those events used to be optional. Now the pressure can be crazy-making.

Is There an Answer?

Does it have to be this way? No, but ***you will need to swim upstream to achieve writing peace in today's technological world.***

I encourage you to think about this early in your career before you get too caught up in the madness. Decide for yourself how much time you want to spend on marketing, and stick to that limit. Decide which things you might enjoy most, and try them. DON'T TRY TO DO EVERYTHING, at least not until you're richly famous and can (like several authors I know) afford to hire full-time employees to handle all the marketing and publicity.

Crunch Times
Don't let the Internet or marketing or "building a platform" rob you of the time you need to write or make you think you have to hurry, hurry, *hurry* to get your book out there. I think that accounts for a lot of the self-publishing frenzy in recent years. *Slow down!* Enjoy your writing life. Slow and steady—inch by inch—still wins the race. And it gives you time to enjoy your entire life along the way.

What about the times when you just can't slow down, or you won't meet a deadline? I've been caught there plenty of times myself. However, my early "crunch time" behaviors set me back instead of moving me forward. (e.g., I often gave up eating healthy meals and grabbed caffeine-laden soft drinks and chocolate to get me by.)

But since the definition of insanity is doing the same thing over and over while expecting different results, I decided to change my crunch time behaviors. As it turned out, these habits worked so well that I made them a permanent part of my days.

- **Never sit and stare at a blank screen.** When you hit a mental block, get up and move. Do a household chore you hate until you think of something to write next. There is *nothing* in this world that jogs my writing block loose like scrubbing a toilet. It is one of the writer's best kept secrets.
- **Close down email during the day.** Check for emergency email first thing in the morning, answer any from editors, and leave the rest till the end of the writing day. Same goes for turning on the answering machine and returning calls late in the day. If possible, work on a computer with no Internet connection at all. Move the Internet away from your writing space.
- **Keep up with health routines.** Although my brain says, "Skip your run and get to work" or "grab that candy bar and keep working," it never helps in the long run. I am much more productive during busy times if I continue with my 6 a.m. run, eat my oatmeal (ugh), drink my eight glasses of water, and take breaks for healthy meals.
- **Remember to stretch your neck and back.** Because I've

had several neck surgeries, I set a timer for ten minutes throughout my work hours. Every ten minutes I stop and do neck rolls, side bends, and back stretches. This only takes a few seconds, but it lengthens the amount of time I can stay at the computer and lets me finish a work day without headaches and backaches. Every single time that I skip the exercises to save writing time, I pay later by having to quit early and having headaches interrupt my sleep.

• **Give yourself a reward.** Create little rewards throughout the writing day (like ten minutes of reading your favorite mystery for every hour you write) and rewards at the end of the day (a favorite DVD or dinner with a friend). I used to think rewards were silly and childish. Who knows? Maybe they are—but they work!

Slow down most days. Enjoy your writing. Be healthy. And you *will* get the writing done.

Undo It Yourself

"A bad habit never disappears miraculously; it's an undo-it-yourself project."
—*Abigail Van Buren*

We all have some self-defeating behaviors, and sometimes these behaviors can cause our writing dreams to be grounded. Through my years of writing, I certainly developed some bad habits that are counter-productive to my writing. I'm still working to break a few, but most of them are a thing of the past. (I must admit that several of them resurrect and revisit me regularly!) We all have those habits, but no matter how or why we acquired them, breaking them is an *UN*do-it-yourself project.

> There will *always* be reasons not to write—college classes keep you too busy, babies keep you awake, day jobs take your time, teen-agers take your energy, or elderly parents require attention. There will always be reasons to feel depressed about writing: rejections, lack of family support, or poor economic predictions.
>
> It can be good to analyze *why* you're not writing. Obviously, if you can't pinpoint the problem, you will have trouble fixing it. While it's good to know the reasons, though, don't let them become an *excuse* to stay in your miserable non-writing rut.

Reasons or Excuses?

Quite often I hear a list of reasons why a writer isn't writing much—or doesn't plan to get serious about her writing until a future time. You know, that fantasy we all harbor somewhere deep inside about endless uninterrupted hours of quiet, someone else fixing the meals, and words flowing like water.

Plow Past the Problem

Find a way to get past it. Talk to friends. Learn more about your craft. Set goals and deadlines. Take action. For example, yesterday I finally realized that my restless ants-in-the-pants feeling in my office was nothing more serious than the fact that I had piles of books and magazines everywhere. I don't create well in chaos, but I'd run out of room. Solution? A new book case and instant organization. The restless block magically disappeared.

Two years ago I took Margie Lawson's online course called "Defeating Self-Defeating Behaviors." I was physically and mentally dragging and had been for nearly a year, thinking my writing life was about over. The only self-defeating habits I uncovered were severe sleep deprivation, a need for more stretching-type exercise, and a need to give up chocolate and sugar. (I had expected work-related habits to show up, but nope! Just health issues.)

I bit the bullet and kept careful records, promising myself at the end of thirty days that I would go back to the chocolate. I just needed to know if it was honestly contributing to my lethargy and headaches. (Oh, how I hoped and prayed it wasn't so!!!) Well, it was . . .

I had a bad habit of eating sweets for rewards and pick-me-ups and comfort after rejections. I stayed up too late reading (while eating chocolate), and I always thought stretching exercises like gentle yoga were a waste of time. Wrong on all counts! Each one was a big factor in the daily headaches, which I'd had for years, and I eliminated a lot of the pain in those thirty days!

No More Excuses

Breaking those three bad habits became my "undo-it-yourself" projects. Was it fun? No—especially going without chocolate. But after the first week, I sure didn't miss it like I thought I would. The habits (dare I say excuses?) that interfere with your writing dreams won't be the same as mine, but I can guarantee you one thing. Breaking those habits is going to ultimately be your own "*UN*do-it-yourself" project.

It's *your* life. It's *your* writing life. No one will create the writing life of your dreams for you. It will require effort of your own—and lots of it. So what are you going to do with your bad writing habits that are holding you back and stealing your dream?

My advice is a paraphrased Nike slogan: **Just Undo It!**

Timing Is Everything

Many times we get to the end of a day and are disappointed at the amount of writing we accomplished. We were busy—so where did the time go? That is the $64,000 question. And in order to get more writing done, it needs an answer.

A common suggestion for getting a grip on how you spend your days is to use a timer (manual or computer) to gather information first. Here's the process to do that, and it will ultimately help you get more writing done.

Where'd the Time Go?
When making your daily goal (or to-do) lists, try to estimate how long you think a task will take. Then time yourself while you do each task. After timing it, write down how long the task actually took to complete. Do this for a week or so. The first time I did this, boy, was I surprised!

A few tasks that I allowed half an hour took only fifteen minutes by the clock. However, the opposite was almost always true. Even though I'm considered a fast writer, the projects I allowed thirty minutes for usually ended up taking an hour or more. (This phenomenon of estimations being way off is similar to how people trying to lose weight generally over-estimate how many calories they burn in exercise and under-estimate how many calories they eat.)

Caution!
The timer is your friend—so don't let it become a tyrant for you.

Now that I know about how long a writing task should take, I schedule that amount of time and use the timer to count down the minutes. If the timer is running, for example, while I write my blog, I see it ticking away and am much less likely to be distracted by email or Facebook (unless I finish with a few minutes to spare).

Don't let the timer become your new tyrant though. No need to hyperventilate as the minutes slip away. *Don't let this timer become your enemy, just one more pressure that you don't need.* Instead, tell yourself that the timer is a friend encouraging you to make the best use of your time, to feel good about what you have accomplished at the end of the day.

> After timing myself, it quickly became apparent why I ended most of my writing days feeling like a failure. I was trying to squeeze twelve hours of work into eight. I couldn't do it, no matter how much I pushed myself. But I learned some very valuable information for future planning. By making more realistic to-do lists, I got rid of much frustration and stopped ending each day disappointed.

Build in Cushion Time

There is one additional way to take the pressure off. I used to schedule every minute of the day, eating breakfast and lunch at my desk. Now I don't. Instead, I leave a full unscheduled hour, scheduling only seven hours of work for an eight-hour day, for example. I know that things will sometimes go wrong, emergency phone calls will come, or there will be a computer glitch. In other words, I leave unscheduled open time each day.

I use the timer faithfully. IF I get to the end of the day without using up (or frittering away) that cushion of time, I can use it however I want. If my eyes are still able to focus, that usually means reading a good mystery. Otherwise it's a good English movie (preferably Jane Austen), a walk, or listening to a book on tape. If you enjoy surfing the 'Net, you could do that now too.

All Stages of Life

When I started writing years ago, I only had one hour per day (nap time) to devote to writing. As the kids got older, it stretched to two hours (nap plus "Sesame Street"). I timed both things. This "count-down" timer technique works to help you get more done with less frustration, no matter how much time you have for your writing at this moment.

It's also a habit that will help you be more productive once your available hours increase. Otherwise, as many full-time writers will tell you, your tasks just expand to fill your available time, without getting much more done at all!

Email: The Hidden Enemy

Statistics from a couple of recent studies shocked me. The effects of checking email are more detrimental to writers than just the time that is wasted. It can interrupt your creative flow so often that you quit writing for the day.

Serious Problem for Writers

In a study cited in "Email Becomes a Dangerous Distraction" an article that appearead in the *Sydney Morning Herald* (Sept 9, 2008), you can see the problem is a real danger:

> *In a study last year, Dr. Thomas Jackson of Loughborough University, England, found that it takes an average of 64 seconds to recover your train of thought after interruption by email . . . It had been assumed that email doesn't cause interruptions because the recipient chooses when to check for and respond to email. But Dr. Jackson found that people tend to respond to email as it arrives, taking an average of only one minute and 44 seconds to act upon a new email notification; 70% of alerts got a reaction within six seconds. That's faster than letting the phone ring three times.*

The findings astounded me, and at first I didn't believe them. But then I caught myself doing exactly what the article said. I used to write the blog first thing in the morning. It was on my schedule to do from 6 to 7 a.m. After that came my book writing. But I rarely actually STARTED the blog till 7 a.m. Why?

You guessed it: checking and answering email. I started with the two or three that were legitimately important to deal with. Ten minutes were needed—tops. But during that ten minutes, others popped up—not important ones. I knew it would take "just a few minutes" to deal with them and get them out of the way. So I did that. And read a few more . . . The next time I checked, an hour had passed.

Tip of the Iceberg
According to the article, the lost time dealing with unimportant emails and deleting spam (and checking your spam folder thoroughly because one of your kids' emails always ends up there) is just the tip of the iceberg. It's the rest of the iceberg that is *critical* to writers.

> *. . . it takes an average of 64 seconds to recover your train of thought after interruption by email . . .*

If the average email checker takes 64 seconds to recover her train of thought, I'm guessing that the average creative writer takes longer than that. For fiction especially, you have to take time to re-enter your pretend world. You have to re-immerse yourself in your characters, the setting, the problem, and the emotional place in the current scene.

It wouldn't surprise me, if you're writing fiction, if it takes double that time to fully recover your train of thought. Think of the time wasted! The flow interrupted! Even more, consider how much harder we are making it on ourselves as writers.

Getting Started Again and Again
Nearly every writer from the beginning of time has agreed that the hardest part of writing is getting started. If you check email even four times per hour (much less than the average computer worker), you have to go through the "getting started" agony four times instead of just once. You have four times as much chance that you'll quit writing during that hour. Who wants to keep "getting started" during their entire writing time?

You think you don't check email that often? Consider this point made in "Email Becomes a Dangerous Distraction:"

> *"Dr. Karen Renaud, a lecturer at the University of the*

West of Scotland, and her team discovered that while 64% of respondents claimed to check their email once an hour, and 35% said they checked every 15 minutes, they were actually checking it much more frequently, about once every five minutes. For some people, checking email is no longer a conscious and deliberate act, but a compulsion they are barely aware of." One author later goes on to compare the compulsion associated with email to people playing slot machines. Ouch!

According to Dr. Renaud, "email users fall into three categories: relaxed, driven, and stressed." The *relaxed* user gets to email when she gets to it, much like regular snail mail. *Driven* email users are managing to stay on top of things, but they feel driven to do so. The *stressed* email users feel the pressure of email piling up, and it takes a negative toll on their emotions and productivity. (I think I'm in the "driven" category.)

Take Control of Email Interruptions

Writers would do themselves a big favor if they moved to the "relaxed user" category. And if that appears impossible to do during your writing time, you can do what I do. I write on a desktop computer not connected to the Internet. I remove the laptop (with Internet) to another room. I don't have email on my phone. Sometimes I even go somewhere and write longhand. I try to remove easy access to email (and related distractions like Facebook and Twitter).

If email (and other Internet distractions) are robbing you of writing time, get tough on yourself about it. Drastic times call for drastic measures!

Finding Time: Pruning Before Prioritizing

According to time management experts (or "time analyzers") the average American spends, in his lifetime, three years in meetings, 1,086 "sick" days in bed, eight months opening junk mail, seventeen months drinking coffee and soda, two years on the telephone, twelve years watching TV, three years shopping, one year looking for misplaced items, five years waiting in line, and nine months sitting in traffic.

So much wasted time! Time we could spend writing!

Scrutinize, Then Prioritize

To get organized, we are told to make a list of everything that needs doing, then prioritize. Mark them A, B, and C, or 1, 2, and 3. Do first things first.

Good advice, but there's one critical step before that: *prune the list.* Don't spend time prioritizing unnecessary activity that could simply be eliminated. Some (like opening junk mail) can be cut by 95% immediately. Just throw it away. Other things only require simple adjustments. For example, cut waiting-in-line time drastically by going to banks and grocery stores in non-peak/non-waiting times—and be sure to carry something to work on or read for when you *do* have to wait.

Try a Time Diary

Take a close look at how you spend your time. What can you cut from your list or drastically reduce? *Nothing*, you say? You're already trimmed to the bone? That's what I always said too—till I actually kept a "time diary" for a week, noting how I actually spent my hours. Just like writing down what you really eat in a day can stun you when you add up the actual calories, so can writing down how your time is spent shock you into making changes.

Me? Too Much TV?

For example, I don't watch TV. Haven't liked TV since the '60s. I don't even know what shows are on anymore, nor do I care. So imagine my shock when I wrote down my daily time expenditures to discover that from Monday to Friday I watched two hours of TV daily without fail! Two!

I had been claiming for years—and meaning it—that I didn't watch TV and what a time waster it was. But after I discovered a station that carried all my favorite old shows, I had fallen into the habit of watching "Perry Mason" reruns during lunch. (I finished eating in fifteen minutes, but the show lasted a full hour, so of course I had to see how Perry managed to win his case.) Then I watched "Diagnosis Murder" reruns before going to bed. Ten hours each week! Imagine the writing I could have accomplished in those hours.

I needed to reframe my thinking: my lunch breaks were only refueling stops, not the entertainment hour. And that hour before bed could be put to better use by reading.

My point? Until you write down how you actually spend your time, you may deceive yourself in much the same way as the dieter who doesn't eat junk food but liberally samples every dish before it's put on the table. We are so good at deceiving ourselves!

An Ounce of Prevention

The average person spends 1,086 "sick" days in a lifetime? That's three *years* of your life! If that's truly the case, then now is the time for preventative care.

An hour or two each year spent on my annual physical can spot early problems and save me untold hours/days/weeks later for tests and treatments. The same holds true for my dental checkups. In the past, I skipped dental appointments until the "sensitivity to cold" became an abscessed molar requiring a root canal. Huge expense of both time and money, and so unnecessary!

Learn about what health issues to watch for at your age. Be

prepared. Don't wait till you have curvature of the spine—take extra calcium now. Don't wait till you rupture a disk. Lose the weight now. Don't wait till you have lung cancer. Quit smoking now. Do whatever is necessary TODAY to reclaim for yourself days in the future you are otherwise destined to spend "sick."

Pure Time Wasters

The average person spends eight months opening junk mail and junk email? Discipline yourself starting today to toss it in the wastebasket (or delete it) unopened. Ninety percent of the time, you can tell from the outside of the envelope (or email subject line) what's junk and what isn't. Trash both kinds quickly. Learn about spam filters.

We spend seventeen months drinking coffee and soft drinks? Give them up! They aren't even good for you. Or limit yourself to a cup in the morning and one in the evening, before and after work. It's primarily the coffee and soda breaks *during* work that eat up that time. Fixing the coffee, buying the coffee and soda, drinking it, wiping it up, cleaning cups, going back and forth from the break room and chatting along the way—all huge time wasters. Keep a big bottle of water at your desk instead. It's better for you anyway.

Get Organized NOW

What about all that time spent dressing, shopping, and finding things? Organization would help all three areas. Clean your office and desk and keep it clean with a five-minute pickup before quitting for the evening.

Clean your closets, tossing clothes that don't fit or you never wear. Keep shoes and accessories in good repair so you can grab, dress, and run. Stick lists for groceries and miscellaneous needs on your refrigerator. When the lists are full, combine trips and save time and money.

Buy what's on your list and resist "browsing" in the mall. Browsing is purely for entertainment or sociability, and if you truly love shopping, save it for your weekend entertainment. But don't kid yourself that leisurely shopping, or hunting all morning for the best bargains, does anything but waste time.

Set Boundaries

The average person spends two years of her lifetime on the phone? (Knowing our teens, we might argue that this is a very low estimate!) Know your weaknesses where interruptions are concerned. I have a terrible time getting off the phone when interrupted, so I need to use my answering machine. On the other hand, I can answer the doorbell when it rings because I have no trouble at all telling people who show up that I'm working.

I have a writing friend with the opposite problem. When the phone rings, she takes ten seconds to announce that "this isn't a good time" and gives no other explanation. However, when door-to-door salesmen show up, she gets roped into having her carpet cleaned and pots scoured as products are pushed. The point? *Know your own weaknesses, set appropriate boundaries, and find a way to eliminate the temptations.*

Early Birds Get Extra Time

Are you prone to oversleeping? Do you open one eye, hit the remote control "just to catch the news," and then lie in bed an hour? The early bird still does catch the worm, and people the world over will tell you that if you want uninterrupted time to work, get to your desk early, before the rest of the world wakes up.

Skip the news and reading the paper in the morning. Your day will probably be better for it! If you don't find out till evening about the latest politician's escapade or where Elvis was last sighted, your day will be just as successful.

> Don't waste time prioritizing activities that need to be pruned from your life. Go back and take another look at that time analyzer's list. Be honest and take a *hard* look. You could gain back years of your life by either eliminating or cutting back on several categories.

Remember: Prune First

Keep a time diary for a week or two. Find the time leaks and plug them. Turn that found time into writing time. At the end of your life, instead of twelve years spent watching TV, perhaps you will have spent twenty years writing—and three years signing autographs!

Procrastination: Have You Tried an Unschedule?

Last week I tried the "Unschedule," a technique for breaking through procrastination found in Neil Fiore's book, *The Now Habit*. The four days that I used Fiore's "unschedule" turned out to be some of the most productive I've had in a while. The one day I disregarded it (thinking I really don't have time for these breaks—too much to do) I actually got *less* work accomplished!

This coming week is very full again. I'm tempted—again—to scrap the Unschedule as a bit "frivolous," but then I remember last Thursday. I dumped it that day too—and got precious little done and didn't even enjoy the time off. So . . . I filled out my Unschedule this morning before starting work.

What in heaven's name is an Unschedule?

Hooked on Play

A clue is on the cover of the book. The full title of Fiore's book includes the subtitle: *A Strategic Program for Overcoming Procrastination and Enjoying Guilt-Free Play*. An unschedule is a way that incorporates play and leisure FIRST in your schedule. Yes, you actually put FUN on your schedule before your chores are listed. Each immediate and frequent reward follows a short (thirty minute) period of work. This is instead of delaying a reward until the whole project is done or until you've written the entire morning.

For example, last week I had a five-hour critique to do. Always in the past, I did the five hours non-stop, then crashed with a bad neck ache and headache that ruined the evening. Last week I scheduled it in smaller chunks with rewards interspersed frequently. I finished the day feeling physically well and mentally upbeat—with the work done.

Why Fun First?
We're trying to overcome procrastination here—getting previously frozen people back to writing, enhancing their productivity and creativity. Fiore says:

> "By starting with the scheduling of recreation, leisure, and quality time with friends, the Unschedule avoids one of the traps of typical programs for overcoming procrastination that begin with the scheduling of work—thereby generating an immediate image of a life devoid of fun and freedom. Instead, the Unschedule reverses this process, beginning with an image of play and guarantee of your leisure time."

Before scheduling the fun times, block out the chunks already committed elsewhere—taking kids to ball practice, a class you teach, lunch, etc. It will encourage you to get started a bit quicker when you see how much free time you *actually* have (or don't) for your writing.

Tiny Work Loads
The other recommendation for the Unschedule is to keep work periods to thirty minutes. Thirty **UN**interrupted minutes. Thirty minutes of work—use a timer to be sure—and it can't include anything like checking email on a whim, or returning a phone call, or other distractions we procrastinators are famous for. If you do that, re-set your timer and start over to clock in thirty uninterrupted minutes.

After your thirty minute period is up, record the actual work done on your daily schedule and then freely enjoy your reward. Fiore advises,

> "Thirty minutes reduces work to small, manageable, rewardable chunks that lessen the likelihood that you will feel overwhelmed by the complexity and length of large or menacing projects."

Believe it or not, thirty minutes of concentrated writing can mean a lot of pages piling up by the end of the day. If getting started is a problem for you, at least give it a try. I find the system so enjoyable that I doubt I'll ever go back to being my former slave driver boss!

The Power of Writing Things Down

I was shocked to discover that I had high cholesterol. It's been low all my life, so I quickly agreed to try a very low fat diet for three months to see if I could bring it down without medication. I religiously wrote down each morsel I ate, along with the grams of saturated fat, trans fat, etc. for each item.

Just having to write things down has helped me make good choices. I definitely prefer Cheetos®, but the nutritional information on the package was alarming. An apple with cheese (fat-free!) suited my goals better.

Does this have anything to do with writing? Yes, it does. The power of writing things down is amazing!

Trackers Are Winners

My best friend lost 100 pounds six years ago, and she's been able to *keep it off.* That puts her in the top 5% of people who lose weight. She now leads a recovery group helping others lose excess weight. When I asked her for some secrets of her self-discipline, she mentioned that she kept careful written track of the food she ate—daily.

Even six years later, she still tracks her food intake, like the others in the top 5%. What's the power in writing things down? She didn't know, but several big studies have shown that dieters who *write things down* lose twice as much weight.

So, you're still wondering, what does this have to do with writing?

Keeping Track

I believe that action of *writing things down* works to help us attain our writing goals as well. There are many kinds of writing schedules (or systems) you can choose from. I'll share what has worked for me.

Currently I use the "write thirty minutes and then reward yourself" system. I keep track of the minutes I actually write. Each time I work thirty **UN**interrupted minutes, I can log it in. I only keep track of hours written on my current novel, time writing the blog I'm paid to write, time studying a writing book, and time spent on my marketing efforts. I do **NOT** count reading or answering email or surfing the 'Net or reading other people's blogs. Even though it can be tiring and email needs to be done, it doesn't get tracked as "writing work."

The days I keep track and write down what I accomplish are days when I write more and accomplish more. I don't honestly know why, but it's true. Do you suppose the parallel holds with the dieters?

Would keeping track of our progress DAILY help us write twice as much—as dieters lose twice as much? Would it help us establish habits that will sustain us in the long run? Is that how the top 5% of writers who actually make a living at their writing manage to do it? The similarities bear thinking about!

> I encourage you test out the power of writing things down. Choose a notebook or journal (or a spreadsheet, if you prefer) and make a "work journal." Have an official place where you *daily* write down the time spent on each writing activity. Use a timer to be accurate.

Don't burden yourself with goals for a while. Simply write down every bit of writing you do in a twenty-four hour period. It will certainly make you aware of how much you write (or don't write.) Put this idea to the test. You also may be amazed at the power in writing things down.

Course Corrections

I recently read that the trajectory of the successful Apollo moon rocket was "off course" 90% of its flight—yet it still reached the moon!

How did that happen?

   1) Scientists acknowledged the deviations from the expected path.
   2) They repeatedly made the *necessary course corrections.*
   3) They achieved an adequate (though not perfect) trajectory to the moon.

Scientists made a major breakthrough in space exploration by sticking to the mission *in spite of* numerous and continual setbacks.

How's *Your* Trajectory?

What does the moon mission have to do with writing?

Well, I was looking at my yearly goals, and like the Apollo mission, my trajectory is off course for meeting those goals—and has been most of the year. Earlier I made enough course corrections to help, but over the summer my trajectory got way off! In the past, my strategy for reaching goals has been to first make them, then get *waaaay* behind or detoured, then either give up on the goal, or make drastic course corrections to force myself back in line.

The drastic course corrections usually happened when I had a deadline with a publisher. For example, the original goal might have been to write five pages per day for four months. Not hard. However, after procrastinating for two months, I would panic, course correct my goals, and commit to writing *ten* pages per day to meet the deadline. That writing schedule worked until Day Four when an interruption kept me from the keyboard.

What's the Answer?

Now, *right there*, an Apollo scientist would have immediately refigured the goal, spreading out that minor missed day of writing over the coming weeks. But I tended instead to let one day of failure slip into two or three. Denial is a great place to live—as long as you can afford to stay there!

But eventually panic sets in, and you are forced because of the deadline to refigure your trajectory again. By now, though, you have to write 15-20 pages per day to make it. *Every day.* No days off.

Panic and adrenaline can manage it, to the detriment of your health and the quality of your writing. How much better off I would always be if I followed the successful Apollo mission method instead.

Keeping Track

Here is where a spreadsheet would help. The very day you fall behind your goal, you could refigure your daily word counts. One day's lost writing spread out over the coming weeks would barely be noticed. Regaining the path to your deadline would take very little extra daily effort. And if, *every single time* you got off course, you refigured and kept moving, you'd also hit your target.

> We need to learn to be resilient instead of panic or live in denial. Every time we have a setback, we need to recalculate. A setback requiring a course correction might come in the form of being sick yourself, having a child needing extra help, unexpected company arriving, you name it! Life is full of things that cause setbacks for writers. Any number of things can push you off your trajectory.

Monitor Carefully

We may not be flying to the moon, but we can learn a lot from this successful Apollo mission that was off course most of its flight. We need to pay attention to our goals and our progress, be aware when we're off course, and make those corrections quickly.

This skill is a part of the successful—and *sane*—writer's life.

A Writer's Emotions

Write What You Love

Several years ago a book by Marsha Sinetar, *Do What You Love, The Money Will Follow*, intrigued me with its title. This subject sparks controversy among writers—and I've had mixed feelings about it myself sometimes.

Perhaps you think you're already doing what you love—writing—and hoping the money will follow. *But are you truly doing what you love?* Are you writing the story or article or book that you yearn to write? Or have you settled for writing about hot topics or following a current trend or only submitting what's listed in the market books? If so, you may develop money troubles in the long run.

To be successful as a writer—to make a living—I would paraphrase Ms. Sinetar's title to say, "Write what you love, and the money will (probably) follow."

The Passion Factor

"Become aware of the passion factor," says Richard Carlson in *Don't Worry, Make Money*. Critical to our success, he says, "passion is a virtually unstoppable, attitudinal force that generates energy, creativity, and productivity . . . Part of the process of creating passion in your work is choosing *work that you truly love*." [emphasis mine]

Can you *really* make money by writing what you love? How do the elements of this "passion factor" increase your moneymaking potential?

When you write what you love:

You're eager to start work each day. You hit the floor running, not because your rent is due or because you're on a tight deadline, but because you *want* to. Your rent certainly might be due, and the deadline might be tight, but this isn't the driving force that propels you to your computer. *This difference cannot be over-emphasized.*

This eagerness to work is what carries you through your projects to completion. Such enthusiasm sweeps you along (on good writing days and bad) from the conception of your writing idea, through the rough drafts and many revisions, and keeps you "pumped" until you finish the manuscript and mail it.

> Excitement and enthusiasm are often absent when you're working on what you believe is merely a "hot topic." It can be like pulling teeth to get started each day. Many such writing projects languish half-finished in a desk drawer when enthusiasm fades midway. Finishing the manuscript to submit and sell is much more likely when your writing is fueled by passion and excitement.

You will automatically work more hours, take fewer breaks, and stop wasting time. Besides getting to work sooner and with more eagerness when you write what you love, you will also work harder once you start. When I'm writing something that I've chosen simply because I have bills to pay, I do finish the manuscript— punctuated by numerous trips to check the refrigerator, email, Facebook, and the mail box. I watch the clock ("Isn't it time to quit yet?") and sigh a lot. My mind is fragmented; I waste a lot of work time.

Contrast that with a project that I've been wanting to do for several years and finally had the chance. Once the house is quiet, I sit down at my computer and write and polish for hours. Most days I snack every hour or two, but when working on something I'm excited about, I ignore my first signs of hunger, then work on until the stomach growling can't be ignored. I can often quit early for the day because I make such good use of my time. *And making good use of your writing time means finishing more manuscripts and making more money.*

Your unique "voice"—what sets you apart in the markets—is easier to find when you're passionate about your writing. When writing on trendy topics, on the other hand, we try to make our voice acceptable to the masses. It's the difference between giving an acceptance speech to a crowd of strangers, and telling your best friend about your freak car accident. The acceptance speech will probably be "formal," lacking that special "fingerprint" identifying you. However, your true voice—its idioms, expressions, word twists, unique phrases—will come through in your enthusiastic tale to your best friend.

Editors continually search for "new voices." A unique voice is more marketable. You will have little trouble writing in your own unique voice if you write about what truly inspires and interests you. For example, contrast writing a description of your daughter when she curls up in your lap at bedtime to writing a description of the pipes under the bathroom sink. Which one will have the warmth and tone of your own special voice?

Writing what you love will produce your most salable, profitable work. Of my forty-two novels and nonfiction books, my biggest moneymakers (in terms of awards, book clubs, and reprints) were those books I really wanted to write. My enthusiasm never waned during the completion of these projects. They were also my *easiest* books to write. Since those themes and experiences ran deep, I felt as if I were really contributing to good books for children.

Do It Now!

Writing what you love appeals to your heart and soul, but it's also the most practical way to make money. It's not something to save for the future, after you've proven yourself as a writer. Writing what you love is not something just for writers who are independently wealthy or have a spouse to support them financially. Writing what you love—what you feel passionate about—is your most practical way to increase your writing income. It's not a luxury—in my opinion—but a necessity.

Without passion, your odds of success are smaller. Your writing career will often seem like a struggle, if you don't burn out completely. But when passion for your work fills your heart and you take the time (and courage) to discover what is truly nourishing to your soul, an abundant writing life can be yours.

So take a chance. Pursue your passions in your writing. If you can't afford to do this full-time, split your writing time between "have-to" projects and ones dear to your heart. See if, in the long run, you don't write better (and more) by writing what you love.

Facing Your Creative Fears

"Every tomorrow has two handles, we can take hold of it with the handle of anxiety or the handle of faith."
—*Henry Ward Beecher*

All of our writing tomorrows give us that very same choice. Do we face our blank computer screens or empty tablets with fear or with faith? Faith encourages us and spurs us on. Fears paralyze—and need to be dealt with. Writing anxiety comes in many forms and develops for a variety of reasons. If we harbor writing fears, how can we identify and eliminate them, then regain faith in our writing tomorrows?

Dealing with creative fears generally involves a three-part process.

First, identify the fears. Otherwise you're only shadow boxing. What are you afraid of? That your ideas are stupid or overdone? That you don't have the talent to be a published writer? That your friends or family will ridicule you when they find out what you're trying to do? That you'll be rejected? That you'll be wasting your time; that being a writer is just a dream that will dissolve in the face of reality? That you'll never be more than a mid-list author on the brink of oblivion?

Second, if your fears are just myths, debunk them. Write down and study your list of fears. Will your husband/wife really laugh at you for wanting to write? Do you really not have *any* talent? (What about your writing teacher or critique partner who loves your stories?) In *The Courage to Write*, Ralph Keyes says, "All writers must confront their fears eventually. The sooner they do this, the better their work will be."

Besides, if you don't, you'll go from fearful to blocked to *frozen*, then give up. Quitting is failing. While none of us may ever totally conquer our writing fears—and some experts say that this writing "anxiety" is actually indispensable writing energy—we can rise above the fears sufficiently so that we can work.

And in doing the work, day in and day out, the fears begin to dissolve. They become like the monster we were so sure, as children, lurked under our bed. After enough years of NOT being eaten alive at night or being grabbed by the ankles when we jumped out of bed, we finally concluded the monster was in our imagination and forgot about it. Most of your writing fears will go away too IF you face them and feel them—and write anyway.

Writers have many fears, and this realization takes many new authors by surprise. "It's a vital thing to remember both as creative people and those who have the opportunity to nurture the creativity in others: Creativity requires courage!" says Thomas Kinkade in *Lightposts for Living*. "It takes courage to push ourselves off center, to think in nonstandard ways, to journey outside the ruts. It also takes courage to resist the pressure of those who very much prefer to walk in those ruts."

Third, if your fears are real, face them squarely and deal with them. Do you really lack sufficient writing skills? If so, enroll in a course. Study writing books on your own. Analyze the books you love best to see how those authors did what they did. Take a public speaking course if you want to be a storyteller or give talks for groups. Take an assertiveness course or get help for your codependency if nasty family members really are holding you back from trying.

Work to improve, but don't get caught in the "perfection trap" by accident. "It is indeed important to strive for excellence in creative endeavor," says painter Thomas Kinkade. "It's important to grow in skill, improve technique. But if we make a god of perfection, we risk pushing ourselves into a creative desert. We're afraid to try because we're afraid we won't be good."

We're In It Together

"But I *am* afraid!" you say, terror creeping in around the edges of your voice. I know you are. I'll tell you a secret. We all are. We wear masks to hide it, but we all deal with the fear of writing. How? *We learn, finally, to do the writing afraid.* We learn that fear doesn't have to stop us, that most things we can go ahead and do whether we're scared or not.

> We research, even if we're afraid our idea is overdone. We write rough drafts, even when we're afraid the whole thing stinks. We submit to publishers, even though we're afraid that editors cringe when they spot our name on a manuscript. Finally the magic occurs. After many, many repetitions, the fear disperses. It almost disappears.

In *The Courage to Write*, Ralph Keyes said, "Finding the courage to write does not involve erasing or conquering one's fears. Working writers aren't those who have eliminated their anxiety. They are the ones who keep scribbling while their heart races and their stomach churns, and who mail manuscripts with trembling fingers."

A Writer's Job Description

Susan Jeffers wrote a book some years ago called *Feel the Fear and Do It Anyway*. The title says it all. It's okay to feel the emotion of fear; it doesn't mean we have to turn tail and run. If you study Eric Maisel's creativity books, you'll come to believe that the anxiety is actually good, that it's pure energy at your disposal, ready to be harnessed for your creative work. Think of the fear like electricity. You can electrocute yourself with it, or channel it so that you light up a whole city. The fear/energy is the same. Writers need to learn how to use this creative fear energy wisely.

Do It Today!

Don't stay frozen. Tackle those fears. Start small. Celebrate each baby step taken as a victory. Don't hesitate to ask people for advice and encouragement. Study books. Listen to audio tapes. Read articles and newsletters. Make banners or posters for your office. Leave Post-It notes on your computer. Use every means possible to remind yourself that you can conquer the thing that you fear.

You've conquered fears in the past, and you can do it again! Don't let fear stand between you and the writing career of your dreams.

Writer Imaging

Picture this: you're feeling strong and confident. Your writing is going well, you're in the flow. That is, until you see her, that Famous Writer, on the cover of *Writer's Digest* or being interviewed on the "Morning Show." Rejection slips and cash flow crunches are just distant memories to her. Or maybe it happens closer to home. Someone in your writing group sells a series and is suddenly catapulted into living *your* dream: The Perfect Life of a Successful Writer.

Why couldn't this perfect writer's life be yours? Eyes squinted and stomach churning, you'd gladly trade your computer for a slot on the *New York Times* Bestseller list. Or any list, for that matter. No chance, you think glumly. Your self-esteem plummets, you scorn your own wishful thinking, and you reach for the nearest writer's block enhancer: food, drink, TV, Facebook . . . The writing is forgotten for a day or a week . . . or a month.

False Imaging

The above writer is a victim of "writer imaging." Just as young girls and women are subjected daily to air-brushed and computer enhanced images of perfect women that create a distorted body image, writers are exposed via magazines, newspaper interviews, websites, podcasts, and bookstore signings to distorted images of writers. Unless you boycott all media, you can't avoid these images. However, you *can* avoid the other part of the problem: your own (mis)perception and resulting lowered self-esteem.

The Illusion

The writing world focuses on fame, like society focuses on thinness, often to the point of obsession. And "fame" is a relative term. To one writer it means selling a story to *Highlights* so that all her friends will read it in the dentist's office. To another writer, fame is an award, a contract with a big name publisher, or an invitation to speak at a conference.

Media messages associate writing success and fame with the perfect writing life—a better, happier, more successful life. But this false image of perfection falls far short of reality. The promise is an empty one.

The Truth

Biographies and profiles have shown that the attitudes and behaviors shared by happy writers have nothing to do with fame or fortune, just like being a happy woman has nothing to do with being thin and beautiful. Thanks to years of popular mainstream media and entertainment perpetuating the myth, many girls and women have been conditioned to believe that happiness is something only for the thin. And thanks to years of writer profiles in the media, new writers have been conditioned to believe that their contentment depends on publication and sales.

However, according to our most reliable sources—happy writers—the "good writing life" is actually dependent on five "non-fame" conditions:

1) **Actively and intentionally writing every day**, even if it's only a journal entry or your Morning Pages, as promoted by Julia Cameron's *The Artist's Way*. Whether selling or not, most writers are happier when they're writing on a daily basis. Many writers claim that they're better parents, spouses, and friends when they're writing. I can attest to that myself.

2) **Staying organized.** Being able to write daily often depends on our level of organization. When our offices overflow with stacks of unanswered mail, unread newsletters, and scraps of paper everywhere, the messiness often makes us depressed and antsy, unable to sit down and work. We take one look at the mess in the office—and leave.

On the other hand, being organized calms us and makes us want to write. This becomes a daily "happiness habit" after a while. Elaine Fantle Shimberg, in her book *Write Where*

You Live, says organization builds routines. And "routines created to fit your personal schedule and time commitments can quickly become work habits. These habits help you to assume the professional persona as soon as you enter your office space . . . Routines help you prevent sliding into procrastination," which makes us unproductive and miserable.

3) **Staying productive with meaningful work.** When we're working on a project that feels important—something that we know will benefit our readers in some way—we're happier writers. These tend to be stories and books we need to write. It will be a book or article that "in some way speaks profoundly to the core of his [the writer's] beliefs, the emotional and spiritual and intellectual center of his life" (from Philip Gerard's *Writing a Book That Makes a Difference*). When your work is meaningful to you and touches others' lives, you're a happy writer, whether it ever makes you rich and famous or not.

4) **Staying focused on the positive.** View your writing life as a series of opportunities and growth experiences, even though some experiences (like rejection slips) may involve pain. Focus on the excitement of finding a good idea, researching a fascinating subject, or working in a quiet library where you can still smell stacks of actual books.

In the same vein, avoid worry, anger, and depression whenever possible, and if it's a part of your life, *stop and deal with it*. In *The Right to Write*, Julia Cameron says "the truth is that too much torment and too much depression can make it as difficult to write as to make the bed, wash the dishes, do the laundry. To the depressed person, writing may present itself as one more chore. For this reason, we are actually working on our writing when we directly address the larger issue of our happiness."

5) **Spending time socializing with other writers.** Form writing and critique groups. One word of caution, though: choose WORKING writers, not just people who like to talk about writing someday or only go to workshops. Choose writing friends who actually are committed to writing consistently and trying to improve. Iron sharpens iron.

You need to spend time with writers who will hold you accountable, not for sales, but for trying, for studying the markets, for revising, for doing thorough research, for your daily journaling, or whatever writing activities you've chosen for your growth. And if the writers you meet with stop writing, don't feel compelled to remain in the group. Drop out and find other working writers to socialize with. You will help each other along.

The Whole Truth and Nothing But

Believe it or not, winning an award or being the author of Oprah's book club selection would NOT change your writing life, either for better or for worse. That's because fame and fortune (both which are fleeting) are not the elements of a good writing life any more than being thin guarantees happiness for women.

Incorporating the five elements in your life will do a lot more for creating a happy writer. The best part about this news is, of course, *that these five attributes are totally under your control.* They don't depend on the shifting markets, changing times, or fickle public taste. Each attribute of a happy writer's life is attainable by *every* writer.

So start today. *Right now.* Change your perceptions of what a successful writer's life entails. Then go out and make it happen for yourself.

Silent Sabotage

The writing is flowing. You're accomplishing your daily word counts. Then, without warning, you take a nose dive. You spiral downward to crash and burn. Your writing comes to a screeching halt. *Why?*

Silent Sabotage

This phenomenon happens when we least expect it. There are many varieties of silent sabotage. Here are some of the most common forms for writers:

You're doing well on your writing (your output, your class work, your marketing, etc.). Love those productive days! Then a little voice in your head whispers, "You know it'll never last. It never does! It's just a matter of time before you're blocked again. Might as well give up now—you'll never make it."

You plan to write your blog and study online writer's guidelines, but you realize you've been surfing the Web for half an hour of your "writing" time. You only had an hour to write, and you've wasted half of it! How discouraging. A feeling of hopelessness sweeps over you. The voice whispers, "Well, today is blown. You can't get anything done in the little time you have left. Might as well keep surfing."

You've finally finished the story or book manuscript. You've worked hard, and success feels great. What a high! The voice whispers, "You deserve a reward, a break from the computer." So you don't write the next day . . . or the next . . . or the following week or month. Your break turns into a full-blown block, and you just can't get started again.

Voice Message

So what can you do about this silent sabotage, this automatic negative thinking that comes unbidden to your brain? Remember, where the mind goes, the man or woman follows. If you don't want to crash and burn, what voice messages can replace the sabotage?

When things are going well, pat yourself on the back. Remind yourself that "slow and steady wins the race." If you set goals that are truly achievable on any given day, and you persevere day after day, you *will* succeed. You will finish that manuscript; you will submit it (and re-submit if necessary). If you refuse to give up despite rejections, if you are willing to revise, chances are good you will sell it.

> When you've wasted your writing time by playing Solitaire or surfing or writing endless emails to friends, tell yourself (like the dieter who splurged), "Well, today wasn't my best day. I'll make good use of the time that's left. Tomorrow is a new day with no mistakes in it. Today's mistake is limited to today. Tomorrow I will be even more productive." Stop the slide down that slippery slope of failure.

When you've completed a project and feel the need for a break, schedule it. Choose a reasonable length of time (maybe one day for finishing a short story, or a week after finishing a book). On your calendar also schedule the day you intend to get back to writing. Enjoy the time off guilt-free, but gear up mentally for returning to work when the vacation time draws to a close.

Be aware of your thoughts, and counter those negative ones quickly. Change that automatic voice message. Successful writers have learned how to counter the voices of self-sabotage. *You can too!*

Stages of Writing

There are seven predictable stages we pass through with each creative project, notes Dr. Louise DeSalvo in her book, *Writing as a Way of Healing.** We can derail our entire writing process with certain behaviors at each stage. While sometimes stages can overlap, they are distinct stages with separate challenges—and each stage provides a different opportunity for us to grow as writers.

The seven stages are:

- the preparation stage
- the germination stage
- the working stage
- the deepening stage
- the shaping stage
- the completion stage
- the going-public stage

The **preparation stage** is when puzzling ideas and odd images and snippets of conversation drift in and out of our dreams and thoughts. We wonder what they mean, and we're intrigued. At some point we begin to put things down on paper, trying to organize our thoughts, figuring out what form we want to use and possible viewpoints.

How do writers sabotage themselves during the preparation stage? Several ways. They may try to avoid it altogether and just start writing. Another way is by *not* writing down those fleeting thoughts

*[With Dr. DeSalvo's stages as an outline, I expanded on them in light of what it means to all writers, not just people in need of healing.]

we have at odd times. It's not so much that we think we'll remember those thoughts later. It's more because the thought seemed rather silly, certainly insubstantial. We decide at some level that the idea just isn't big enough to pay attention—and so it's lost.

On the other hand, you may take this initial stage so seriously that you shut down. You may expect too much of yourself, thinking that if you were a "real writer," you'd have a plan! You'd know where all these odd bits and pieces floating around your head belong. You expect the images and musings to fit into a pattern much too soon, and this kind of pressure can give you a lovely writer's block before you ever get started.

> In this **preparation stage,** give yourself permission to think and make note of trivial thoughts. Write down everything, no matter how unconnected it might seem to anything you want to write. Eventually, these odd bits and pieces may start making connections and spark other ideas that will be more useful or substantial. Learn to enjoy this stage! Force yourself, if you're a Type A organizational freak like me, to let your brain slowly release ideas to you. Don't force connections immediately. Don't try to make each snippet "mean something."

The **germination stage** is a time when we gather those bits of ideas and trivia and images and scenes and plot ideas and try to figure out where it all might be leading. It can feel confusing. During the germination stage, my Type A personality wants to organize, and yet so much of what occurs to us during this time isn't "organizable" yet.

I used to follow the advice to write down ideas on scraps of paper and stick them in a folder, but I soon found that my own personality hated that. I would open the file folder, see all those scribbled scraps on paper napkins and file cards and the backs of receipts—and it looked like chaos. Chaos of any kind has never been conducive to writing for me. And yet, if you push yourself to organize during the germination phase, you are almost sure to derail any creative impulses trying to emerge.

Is there a solution to getting through this phase and gleaning from it everything you need to start working on your novel? I suspect this is an individual matter, but for me, these tips work to keep me from derailing during this phase:

Follow your urges to read. They will come at such odd moments. You'll be sorting through junk mail or paying bills, and suddenly you see a flyer on how to save on your water bill. Although 99% of the time you pitch this junk unread, today you feel the nudge to read it. Pay attention to your urges to read. (I have thus found careers for certain characters, plot twists, whole subplots, and clues for mysteries.)

The germination stage is a wonderful time to browse in museums, art galleries, antique shops, flea markets, and other places where you can let your mind and eyes roam. Watch what snags your attention and make note of it.

If you feel you must organize (like I do), get a three-ring notebook and those colored divider tabs. (This method has served me well through forty-two books.) Make sections for book and chapter titles, characters, plot ideas, setting, dialogue, and whatever else you're collecting. Continue to write things on scraps of paper as they come to you, but after you have several scraps, sit down with your notebook and add the information behind the correct colored tab. Is it a snippet of dialogue you overheard on the bus that is just perfect? Transfer it to the dialogue section. Did you find an odd fact about 1940s mail carriers? Put it in the character section. Did you read about a bizarre event in the newspaper? Add it to the plot section. None of this is written down in any order, but as your sections fatten with ideas, your mind will (quite unconsciously) start to sort it out and make connections. In a later stage, when you go through the various sections of notes, you'll be amazed at the ideas that will have begun to gel.

Next comes the **working stage**, the one we're probably most familiar with. During this phase we begin our rough draft, build on it, flesh it out, develop our plots and characters, and often fly by the seat of our pants to cross the finish line. Sometimes we see our way clear through this phase, especially if we are voracious outliners.

If you hate outlines, this working stage may be more nebulous as you discover your story. You may get lost and have to start over a few times. But eventually you'll have a rough draft, complete with a beginning, middle, climax and end. You might get the draft critiqued at this point, or you might revise your draft first, smoothing out rough spots, fleshing out the cardboard characters, and building the tension at the climax scene. The working stage is a longer stage, an exciting stage.

What are the dangers during the working stage, the attitudes and behaviors that can derail our writing projects? There are many!

Depending on your personality and favored way of working, you may do some of the following:

- You may slavishly follow your outline instead of your instincts and creative impulses that encourage you to take detours.

- You may derail if you work zealously with high anxiety. Working at a fever pitch, without taking time for relaxation, will cause burn-out and writer's block just from exhaustion.

- If you don't learn to push through the confusion of this stage, you may abandon your project. All rough drafts and early revisions are confusing as you figure out what you're really trying to say, where to put certain scenes and information, and what to do with the new characters and incidents that seem to spring full-blown from your unconscious mind.

- If you are writing your rough draft with your Editorial Mind in gear, you will eventually give up. Editorial Mind is critical, which is a helpful trait later, but judging your work during your rough draft working stage can be lethal.

- If you spend time thinking about the finished product (selling, publishing) when you're trying to write, you won't enjoy the process and you'll be very critical of everything you write. Instead, focus on enjoying the writing process and leave the "product" work until the end (the going-public stage).

At the beginning of the **deepening stage**, you've already completed a rough draft. You may also have done some fixing on your draft, especially if you zipped through the rough draft at lightning speed, just getting it down as fast as you can. You may need to go back, fill in missing parts, and rearrange some things. If you're a writer who writes a bit, then revises that bit before going on, your first finished draft was actually revised as you went along. Either way, it's time to get down to some deeper work now. The deepening stage is more challenging, but very satisfying!

According to Louise DeSalvo in *Writing as a Way of Healing*, in this deepening stage "we revisit, rethink, reimagine, and revise what we've been doing. Often during this stage we learn what our project is really about, even if we've been working on it for years."

There is also a **shaping stage** during which we find the work's form. It may or may not be the form we started with. It might require smaller shaping changes (like shorter chapters), or it might require huge shape shifting (story told from a different viewpoint, story told as a verse novel instead of straight fiction, etc.).

This is hard work, and these stages require a lot of deep thinking. During these stages, I tend to read books about deepening characters, or books on emotional structure and character arcs. I might study books on voice as I rethink various characters and how they're coming across.

The dangers during the deepening and shaping stages have to do with maintaining our interest in the writing project. By now, we may be tired of the story, even sick of it, and the thought of going through the novel one or two or more times makes us want to run screaming into the woods.

If your enthusiasm diminishes, you must find ways to reignite it instead of abandoning the work. Read about the writing processes of other writers. You'll see that you're not alone by any means with the struggles of this stage. And give yourself credit—even celebrate—each new mini-completion you accomplish. It doesn't *feel* like we're making progress—we aren't adding new pages now. However, each time you go through the manuscript and shape a bit here, cut a bit there, deepen that character's motivation, enhance the outdoor scenery, or whatever you feel needs to be done—*you are making progress*. Your project is getting closer to the vision you had way back when you started.

It's a bit like the transition stage of having a baby—you're sick of the whole process and would like to quit and go home—but you're so *close* to holding the baby. Remember that with your book too. The deepening and shaping stages are bringing you ever closer to holding that finished book in your hands.

In the **completion stage**, we go through the book again. We rethink and revise as we get close to the finish line. It's an exciting time, when you feel completely involved in your work again. However, there are dangers to avoid even at this stage.

During the completion stage, you can derail your process several ways:

- If you refuse to let go of your writing project and send it out into the world, your book can fail to be published out of fear. (The "world" can mean your critique partner, your agent, or an editor.) You know in your gut that you've made the book as good as you're able at this point in your learning curve, and that continuing to work on the book is probably not helping it much. In fact, if you keep tinkering needlessly, you can do more harm than good.

- If you lose interest in your work at this point, you may sadly end up putting the manuscript on a shelf in your closet "to work on later," only later never comes. Instead of this solution, you must find ways to rekindle your original enthusiasm for your book. If you kept a work journal for this project, go back and read your original notes and hopes for your book.

- If you become careless during this stage, you might not do the necessary polishing or changing that deep revisions call for. You might settle for a *good enough* manuscript or story, but not rise to the excellence you're capable of at this point in your career. If you find yourself reading through your manuscript and being jolted by certain paragraphs or sentences— yet go on by, hoping no one else will notice the jerky rhythm or unclear sentence—then you're becoming careless. This can derail your project.

It makes no sense to spend weeks, months, or years writing and then, when finishing, to produce a slovenly, careless effort. During the completion stage, you must fine-tune what is there. You must pay attention to detail at this stage. It can be a "slow, meticulous, often plodding process," says Dr. DeSalvo. Yet it is necessary.

"Finishing strong is something great athletes learn . . . Finishing strong is something writers also must learn."

In the **going-public stage** we choose what type of publishing we want and then proceed. For a traditional publisher, the going public stage will involve market study (in market books and online), researching agents (if that's your desire), and submitting the appropriate material requested (a query, a proposal, sample chapters, or the entire manuscript). With so many free self-publishing options for writers now, you might choose to publish an e-book for e-readers or use a POD (print-on-demand) service. These are all viable options for today's writer.

The dangers during the going public stage are getting in a rush. We're tired, we are eager to clear our desks of the clutter, and don't want to think about writing for a while. But writers in a rush make decisions they often regret. They don't do enough research, so they pay thousands of dollars to a rip-off e-publisher or POD publisher when they could have used a free service (like Kindle or CreateSpace on Amazon.com). Writers in a rush are so thrilled when *any* agent responds to their query that they don't fully investigate credentials—and end up with an agent who has no experience and no clout at all in the publishing world. *Do your research.* While taking the traditional-publishing route is definitely slower, you'll end up with an editor, a marketing team, and a sales force to help you. If you self-publish, you're on your own to edit and sell your books. Be honest with yourself. Is that a job you are capable of—and have the time and resources to accomplish?

Whatever publishing route you choose, the going public stage deserves celebration. You've accomplished something very big! Do whatever represents a celebration to *you*. For some, it might be going out on the town. For others, it's a weekend alone to read while your spouse takes the children. It will depend on your personal taste and your bank account, but be sure to choose something that nurtures *you* as a writer. Build yourself up, and soon you'll be eager to enter the preparation stage again!

Sorting Out the Voices

How many voices try to tell you what to write, when to write, and how to write? What voices do you listen to?

Recently I was reading a collection of author profiles titled "Obedient to One Voice" in *Behind the Stories* by Diane Eble. One author (Patricia Sprinkle) talked about her dream to write mystery fiction, but that for six years she wrote anything *but* fiction. She took any assignment that offered to help pay the bills.

> *"And it was a struggle in every way, including financially. But then when I started writing fiction, things began to work out. Again and again, when I choose to do what I truly believe I need to be doing instead of listening to what all the voices around me are saying, God is incredibly faithful in confirming that this is what I need to be doing."*

Sometimes we lose sight of the joy in our work—we can even experience a dreadful writer's block—if we listen to the wrong voices. It's true that we can all learn from others, and we need to be able to take constructive criticism. BUT the voice deciding the course of your career, your subject matter, and how you present it should be *your* voice.

Various Voices

Sometimes we allow voices of parents and other family members to dictate what we should write or judge whether our stories are "good enough." Extremely few relatives are qualified to judge your writing. Parents may be trying to live their dreams through you;

siblings may be jealous. Whether you're fifteen or fifty, you may still be allowing family members to make your writing choices for you.

Sometimes we allow suggestions from our critique group to change our manuscripts, even when their ideas don't ring true at all for us. Or we knuckle under to the more experienced (or outspoken) writer in the group, writing humor (because *he* loves humor) and giving up our historical mystery idea (because historical *anything* is "too hard to sell"). It can be difficult to go against the group opinion, but think carefully before you toss your idea overboard.

Sometimes, like Jane Austen, we're told by publishers and editors (in magazines, at conferences) that certain themes are popular now and make the most money. *Our* desires (our themes and subject matter) now sound old-fashioned or boring. Will we scrap our passion for science fiction set in Italy to write gothic romance in the moors then? Not if you want to enjoy your writing.

> Is there a voice you can trust? Yes, I believe there is. Go back to when the writing bug first bit you. What did you like to write? What subjects intrigued you? What was your writing process like? How did you like to write—barefoot in pajamas, longhand in bed, on a laptop at the library? If you were following your inner voice, you probably experienced a level of excitement about your writing that stands out in your memory.

If you find yourself blocked and uncertain as to what to do, it may be because the voices of other people are drowning out your true writing self. The choice is *always* yours.

Another Voice to Squash

Even after you've made the choice to write, you're not quite done dealing with voices that give you trouble. Does taking time to write make you feel *guilty*? It could be that various people during the course of your life have told you that taking time to write (or just taking time for yourself) is self-indulgent, selfish, or frivolous.

Do you fight your own guilty feelings that say you should be doing something more productive? Does writing—especially if you haven't sold much or aren't making piles of money from it—feel selfish to you? Do the real (or imagined) opinions of others keep you from spending time writing?

The Stages of Guilt

When our children are small, we fight the guilt that comes with motherhood. Are we taking too much time away from the kids? Is it *really* good that they've learned to entertain themselves so well? Is it *really* the responsible thing that my kids are the only ones on the block who know how to run the washing machine and cook meals? Will the children remember Mom as someone without a face, only a hunched back and tapping fingers?

Once my children were grown and on their own, I thought the guilt would stop. But I really identified with Carol J. Rottman in *Writers in the Spirit* when she said:

> *"Now all I have to do is quell my guilt over the things I displace because of my indulgence in writing. There are so many worthy causes that regularly tempt me to leave the desk. A sister describes me as 'driven' when I am so serious about my work, and friends wonder why I don't join them for lunch. My children and young grandchildren, all within a twenty-mile radius, can use as much time as I can give."*

The Cure for Guilt

As in so many cases, the cure for guilt seems to be in finding the right balance. Balance between time for writing and time for family/job/home/community. Have you found the balance that works for you and your family? It will look different if your children are babies than if they're teens or adults.

Consider journaling the answers to these three questions:

- What/who pushes your guilt buttons when you're trying to write?
- How do you choose whether to keep writing or not?
- What questions do you ask yourself in order to find the right balance and keep your priorities straight?

Whether it's deciding to write or not (or *what* to write), we all have to learn to listen to our own hearts. Journal or retreat for a week-end or do whatever is necessary to find the quiet time to do this. If you don't, you'll be following someone else's dream instead of your own.

Conquering the
Green-Eyed Monster

After the war, Scarlet O'Hara starved with her family on their broken down plantation while she burned with jealousy toward anyone who still had money. Later, after marrying Rhett Butler, Scarlet built a gaudy mansion in Atlanta to make her enemies "pea-green with envy" in return. Unfortunately, she found (like many writers) that having people jealous of her success caused her as much heartache as when she was jealous herself.

> *Jealousy. Envy. The green-eyed monster.* Call it what you will, it attacks writers on a regular basis. We don't talk about it much. Sometimes it's just a twinge, like a side ache. Other times it's a full-fledged cramp. It can strike when someone in your writing group sells a story or book, when someone in the chat room writes in glowing terms about recent starred book reviews, when we see that someone's book (that we started and couldn't even finish) made a million bucks as an Oprah selection. Any of these can bring the sting of jealousy.

Other Side of the Coin
On the flip side of the coin, if *our* story just sold or garnered the good review, we can find ourselves stunned, in the position of receiving cold shoulders, raised eyebrows, rejection, and backbiting. This often happens if you finally sell your first manuscript, but your friends haven't sold anything yet. As Bette Midler once said,

"The worst part of success is finding someone who is happy for you."

Frankly, both types of jealousy present challenges, but the second type feels like betrayal, so it can be more difficult to handle. If you're jealous—or others are jealous of your success—there are a number of ways to deal with it. At some point in your writing career, you'll probably have to deal with both kinds.

Tips for Handling Jealousy

First are some ideas for the times when others are jealous of your success. Following that are some suggestions for handling your jealousy of others' success. There are several ways to deal with other people, some kinder and more professional than others!

You can call a spade a spade. Tell them they're jealous and to knock it off and let you enjoy your success. This approach only tends to aggravate the problem though.

If the person listening to your success story is a struggling writer—one genuinely working to write and sell—be sensitive to her feelings. Do share. Be happy, but don't gloat. Don't spend the whole critique period talking about your success. Keep it in balance.

Find a writer who is more published than you are, then shout your success from the rooftops. Do you have an instructor or mentor who's helped you in some way? Those are great people to share good news with, and you can pull out all the stops. They'll be as excited as you are. Nothing thrills me like having a former student get published, and then write to share the news with me.

Brace yourself with certain family members. Jealousy coming from nonwriters (including your family) is trickier, and often the most painful. Family members who were super supportive while you played the Rejection Slip Blues can turn cold when you begin selling. I've never understood this type of jealousy, but I've seen it in my own life and other writers' lives often enough to know it's real. Writers tend to withdraw and shut down when their success stories fall on the deaf ears of family members. Be sensitive to your family issues, but don't let the nonsupport go on too long. Confront it. Your sale or good review is an achievement, and it should be recognized, just as you recognize their accomplishments.

But . . . what if *you're* the jealous one?

Try to distance yourself from the jealousy. Put some space between yourself and the other writer for a moment, and view the event objectively. What can you learn from this writer's success experience? How did she find the right market for her book? How did he help promote his novel so that it got such great publicity? Did they do something you could use to boost your own success? Find the lesson in the experience.

Choose to make that "enemy" into a friend. Rachel Simon, in *The Writer's Survival Guide*, talked about one of her friends, Marianne, who was having great difficulty dealing with the success of another new writer. "The extreme heat of Marianne's envy made her see just how much she wanted to succeed. So Marianne set herself to combating envy with harder work and, instead of seeing her friend as someone to revile, saw her friend as a pioneer leading the way. And so Marianne turned the object of her envy into an object of inspiration."

Instead of focusing on someone else's success, get to work on your own manuscript! Your mind can only concentrate on one thing at a time, the experts tell us, so turn your attention away from the object of your jealousy and address your own writing. Bonnie Friedman agrees in her article, "Envy, the Writer's Disease," that the remedy for jealousy is focusing on your own work. "Not the thinking about it. Not the assessing of it. But the *doing* of it."

Develop a sense of humor. Probably one of the best ways to handle jealousy, if you can muster the courage, is to laugh about it. Laugh about it, you say? Ha! Well, I challenge you to read Anne Lamott's chapter on jealousy in *Bird by Bird* and not laugh out loud. She doesn't pull any punches, but her honesty about the not-so-nice feelings we can harbor about others is so refreshing. "Jealousy is such a direct attack on whatever measure of confidence you've been able to muster," Anne says. "But if you continue to write, you are probably going to have to deal with it, because some wonderful, dazzling successes are going to happen for some of the most awful, angry, undeserving writers you know—people who are, in other words, not you."

So the next time the green-eyed monster takes a chunk out of your hide, remember Scarlet O'Hara's famous line: *"I'll go crazy if I think about that now. I'll think about that tomorrow."* And by the time tomorrow comes, you'll be so involved in your own writing project again that the envy will shrink to its proper proportions.

Give Up Your Perpetual Maybe

Ten years ago, I had a book deadline looming, I was weeks behind, and Christmas was on top of me. More importantly, my oldest daughter's wedding was the day after New Year's. I also had out-of-state siblings coming for a week. Yet the deadline screamed at me to squeeze in time to write during the week they'd be with us.

Oh, in the back of my mind, I knew I'd never pull it off, at least not for more than a few minutes a day. Yet I piled on the "shoulds" and guilt, trying to browbeat myself into working part of the time. Finally, when the internal tension escalated and my ulcer (dormant for months) acted up, I reached a decision. I would say "NO!" to the writing, and I would do it without guilt during the week of the wedding celebration.

Doesn't sound too rebellious, does it? And yet, for most writers, it is.

Don't misunderstand me. The *not working* isn't unusual. We all do that, while pretending that we're going to get to it any minute! We're going to write just as soon as we finish this project, or run the kids to the mall, or help the husband build a deck, or... or...or...

The "no" I'm talking about is something different. I refer to a definite decision NOT to write on a particular day. A decision without guilt! Instead, most blocked writers, procrastinating writers, and wannabe writers live in a constant state of "maybe."

Let Me Be Clear

It's a tense state, never quite working, but always hovering around the edges of the writing. *Maybe I'll write today . . . Well, not right now, maybe later . . .* Never quite writing, but never living the rest of your life either, because to do so would be a definite "no" instead of a "not right now."

For years we've had hammered into us how critical it is to write every day, preferably at the same time each day. I totally agree with this idea—most of the time. But frankly, it can be hard to follow such advice unless we are also able to say a whole-hearted *NO!* to the writing when necessary.

Clearing the Decks

Why is it important to be able to say a definite *no* when you mean not to work?

According to Eric Maisel in *Fearless Creating*, "You must become accustomed to saying no clearly and consciously, so that you can also become accustomed to saying yes." How true!

After the five days of wedding celebration were over and everyone was gone, I took a deep breath. My house was a shambles. I decided to say "no" to the writing one more day in order to take down the drying Christmas tree, clean my office (which had been turned into a guest bedroom) and figure my income taxes. I knew that, with those three things done, I could say an enthusiastic "YES!" to the writing for the rest of the week.

And that's exactly what happened. However, without being able to say "no" when you have to, you can have a string of "maybe" days—and weeks—where nothing gets done and your work is hit or miss.

Signs and Symptoms

Living in a state of *perpetual maybe* is a miserable place for a writer. As Fran Lebowitz once said, "All the time I'm not writing I feel like a criminal. It's horrible to feel felonious every second of the day. It's much more relaxing actually to write." Living in perpetual maybe means a life full of angst, with inner soul struggles that need to be quieted with food or soap operas or a shopping spree. It's a state of confusion and doubt, of hesitation.

Perpetual maybe almost always means an eventual "no." It's a silent "no" that (in my case) might mean a cup of hot chocolate, sending some email, calling a friend, or reading back issues of writers' magazines. It might come close to a "yes" if I spot a potential new market or re-read my story outline. But for all practical purposes, considering the amount of writing that gets done, my "perpetual maybe" is a "no" in disguise.

Hidden Benefits

If all this is true, why would anyone want to stay in the limbo state of "maybe"?

Well, if you secretly mean not to work, but pretend that you will "in just a few minutes," you avoid the anxiety of actually sitting down and trying to pull words out of thin air. You also avoid the guilt associated with deciding that today you won't even try to write.

However, living in perpetual maybe takes its toll. It's depressing. It's debilitating. It destroys self-confidence. It makes *not* writing a daily habit.

The trick, of course, is knowing when you can legitimately say "no" to the writing for the day. You can say no to the writing when something that needs your attention is truly a higher priority. And only you can decide where your priorities lie. Take some quiet time to write them down. During the wedding and holiday time, spending time with my daughter the bride and my out-of-state family was a priority—a once-in-a-lifetime experience.

It's not just the big family things like weddings and funerals that might take priority. It might be a crying child who needs a hug. It might be a friend in crisis. It might be you in desperate need of a nap or hot chicken soup. It might be a date with your wife.

> Learn to be definite in your decisions. Don't let time slip away while you live in perpetual, guilt-producing "maybe." Either decide to write (and get to it) or if something else must take priority, say a definite "no" to the writing for that day. Then attend whole-heartedly (and without guilt) to what needs your attention.

Ready? Set? Say No!

Don't let your writing life slip away as you vacillate in MaybeLand. When you really need to, say a firm *NO* to the writing. You'll be able to say an enthusiastic *YES* that much sooner!

Writing Through the Storms of Life

Writing well requires an enormous amount of concentration and energy, plus a decent dose of self-confidence and courage. It's not like making widgets on an assembly line, where your mind can wander while your hands stay busy producing.

For that reason, even "normal" amounts of stress can freeze your writing fingers. I use normal to mean those stresses that come to us all at times: sick children, fights with a spouse, financial problems, etc. These storms of life are common, but not necessarily easy to ignore so we can write. (For help with more serious issues, see "Writing After Major Losses" about breaking blocks after serious stressors like death, divorce, and job loss on page 133.)

Survival Strategies
To write during normal stressful times, try these techniques to get going:

Inventory your life experiences to create a list of topics to write about. When burned out, or you feel stumped for something to write about, ask yourself questions like, "What has bugged me that I've been able to handle effectively?" or "What have I learned from this experience?" From this come articles that make a difference in people's lives—whether it's teaching them the healing power of laughter or just helping them to decorate on a shoestring.

Then make an inventory of your life experiences. (My first *Writer's First Aid* book has a section called "Getting to Know You," which gives you such an inventory to use.) What have you learned in the school of hard knocks? As writer Marshall Cook said, "You have a great pool of living to dip into for your writing. You've met scores of different people. You've *been* scores of different people." Use that!

Switch from output goals to time goals. At least for a while, switch from a set number of pages per day to hours spent writing. ("I will write for one hour;" not "I will produce five pages.") Skip the daily quota pressure until life settles down, or skip it altogether, as I ended up doing.

Schedule your writing time, but be flexible. Sounds contradictory, but it's not. *Do* schedule writing time, as usual. Strive to keep that appointment, no matter what else is going on in your life. But be flexible; if your time is taken by a bedridden father or an emergency call from your daughter's school, attend to the urgent event, but carve out the writing time later in the day, even if it's in three or four smaller pieces. Overcome the tendency to think, "My writing time is shot today—I'll try again tomorrow."

Develop a specialty. In stressful times, you often become an expert on your situation. Over the years, I've collected extensive libraries on personal recovery, remarriage, writing, quilting, the Civil War, England, and devotional books. You probably have your own collections.

Capitalize on the information you've absorbed. Do more research, and slant ideas many ways: for fiction and nonfiction, for children and adults. For example, if you provide care for a bedridden father, you might write an inspirational piece for adults on having the strength and patience to do it; or a how-to piece for a family magazine on finding the best home health care for an invalid; or a children's article on how to make visits to elderly grandparents a joy to both child and grandparent; or a middle-grade novel that includes living with a bedridden grandparent.

Be yourself. Use your life experiences to express your unique vision of the world and insights into life. Those insights become your style, that special something that is yours alone—*voice.*

Be aware that *all* writers—both the famous and the not-so-famous—deal with stress. They find ways to do this and keep writing, often incorporating those very experiences into their work. Writers write—and not just when the days are easy. We're like postal workers, pushing on through rain, and snow, and sleet, and dark of night . . .

Keep On Keeping On

You're not alone in finding it difficult to write some days. But when the dark days pass, you'll be very glad you continued to work even when it was hard. When the sun comes out again, you'll be thankful that you spent that time growing as a writer. Then it will be full-steam ahead!

Write Your Life—ALL of It!

Writers are told to follow their passion, to write stories and books that move them deeply. Often those very stories come to us in uncomfortable or painful ways, through stressful circumstances in our lives we'd gladly bypass.

Twenty-seven years ago, after my dad died, I tried to finish writing a fun puzzle-type mystery. Even though I'd had several middle-grade mysteries published by then, I just couldn't finish it. Instead, I finally chucked that idea and wrote *The Rose Beyond the Wall*, a middle grade book where the young heroine's favorite grandmother dies from cancer.

Tough Times

I cried when I wrote that book, and I cried when the grandmother died. But the book about how people deal with grief was from the heart. It sold first in hardcover to Atheneum, then to paperback book clubs, and was nominated for several children's choice awards. It's still used in some hospice programs, although it's only available as a reprint from an obscure publisher that brought it back into print ten years ago.

"We may regret our circumstances," says William Stafford, *"and no doubt many of us should. But the way toward a fuller life in the arts must come by way of each person's daily experience."*

Write Through Circumstances

Why use our personal experiences? Our daily lives are full of con-
crete details, raw emotion, lots of issues, drama, and dialogue. It's
a shame not to use it all! And if you want to write authentic, moving stories that ring true, it's the best source of material.

In *Walking on Alligators: a Book of Meditations for Writers*, Susan
Shaughnessy suggested this:

> *"The way to a fuller life in the arts is through your own
> experience today. Many of us are in circumstances no one
> would choose. Loneliness, physical disability, financial want,
> disappointment—we long to escape from these things that
> won't 'let us write.' But we escape by writing right toward
> them and right through them, not by trying to go around."*

Take an Inventory

For the last year or so, there's been something really bugging me
that I can't fix, and it won't go away. I've done everything I can to
just accept it and forget about it—but I can't. I finally realized this
summer that until I fictionalized it and wrote about it, it probably
wouldn't leave me alone. So I'm writing about it now. And believe
me, as heated as the subject makes me, I'm writing this with a lot
of passion!

What's going on in your own life that's unwelcome, yet might lend
itself to a story or novel? Think about your own life, and also the
lives of your children, neighbors, spouse, and friends. What is
causing you (or them) problems today? What about these issues
makes you angry—or sad? What are you learning in your circumstances? Whatever it is, consider writing about it!

Remember: the way to write authentic stories is to write
straight toward them—and through to the other side!

Dealing with Rejections and Setbacks

I imagine it's due to the current economic situation, but several times lately I've been asked if my manuscripts still get rejected. Yes, I still get rejections. Every single writer I know gets rejections—of manuscripts, proposals, queries, you name it. Chances are, if you're never getting rejected, you're not submitting.

Baptism by Fire

I feel for my students who are discouraged over rejection slips; it's a painful period, especially at the beginning! But every career has an apprentice period, and writing is no different. It's like practicing a piano after learning proper techniques—it's how we go from good to improved to even better. Rejections will be frequent until you learn your craft so you can compete in the marketplace.

> You *will* get better! You *will* get rejected less. That's because the best you can write this week will not be the best you can write next week or next month, providing you are writing regularly. But even if you are writing and submitting regularly, there probably will never come a magical time that you don't have to deal with rejections.

Only Temporary—Unless You Quit

Rejections used to depress me a lot. I recall getting five rejections in one day's mail early in my career. You know the doubts that follow. Would I ever sell anything? Was I just chasing rainbows?

Should I go get a "real" job? Even after getting established and selling eleven hardcover books to a top New York publisher, a major setback happened. A recession hit that caused my editor to lose her job and all my books to go out of print within a few months.

Like the economy today, cutbacks were the norm. From 1992-1996, I felt like a has-been and a wash-out, through a five-year period where I sold absolutely nothing. I refused to quit then because I loved to write. I refuse to quit now for the same reason. Although rejection hurts, it's worth it to hang in there.

Dealing with Rejection

One favorite quote about rejections came from Elaine Fantle Shimberg's book *How to Be a Successful Housewife/Writer* retitled as *Write Where You Live: Successful Freelancing at Home.* She said:

> *"There must be a slight masochistic tendency in people who want to be writers. We place our ego in the hands of others while we sit home and wait. And yet, when our work's rejected (it's our work that's being rejected, not us), we don't curse the gods or a distant editor but bounce back up again like those plastic dolls with weighted bottoms that kids use as a punching bag. We do because—that's what writers do."*

Plain and simple. And if you don't own Ralph Keyes' book, *The Writer's Book of Hope,* do yourself a huge favor and get it. After you read his chapters on rejection, you'll never review rejection as "personal" again.

Other Setbacks

> *"The only copy of your manuscript is stolen from your car. Articles and stories come back with unfailing rejection . . . Finances grow ever more perilous. This is, with variations, the script for the first ten or fifteen years of many successful writers' careers. But they hung on."*

This quote comes from one of my favorite book of meditations, *Walking on Alligators: A Book of Meditations for Writers.* It talks about the nearly universal experience of published writers—their successes are interspersed with fairly regular setbacks.

Have you accepted that truth yet?

Re-framing Failure

Even though the overall pattern of your writing experiences will probably be upward (assuming you don't quit), it will be full of ups *and* downs. Ups will include sales and good reviews and awards. The downs—those drops on the chart—include rejections and delays and canceled contracts.

The setbacks are NOT failures or reasons to quit—unless you allow them to be. They're both places of learning and places of rest. They are simply steps on the way to the top. More importantly, they can have a positive effect—if you let them.

Upside of Down Times

Compare it to climbing a mountain. It's usually an up-and-down experience as you work your way to the top. There are periods where you climb upward steadily. Sometimes you also go down— lose a bit of altitude—before starting the next steep climb. Are the downhill stretches failures? No. Setbacks? Not really, although it can feel like that.

Downhill spots have their bright side though. For example, when I "fail" to sell something, it forces me to slow down and ask some questions. And more than one time, the failure to sell a series idea gave me an initial disappointment (lasting about five minutes) followed by a rush of relief that I didn't have to force my exhausted body into another grueling writing stint just yet. The setbacks can be restful, *if we let them be.* They can allow us to recoup some energy instead of draining the last bit we had left.

The periods in our writing life that seem "down" can also be times to rethink and regroup. Maybe we need a course correction. Perhaps that rejection is trying to point us in a new direction in our writing. Or that negative review might be telling us that our real love (and talent) is in writing poetry, not baby board books.

What about when the negatives are too frequent?

> As Harriet Beecher Stowe once said: *"When you get into a tight place and everything goes against you until it seems that you cannot hold on for a minute longer, never give up then, for that is just the place and time that the tide will turn."*

Judging from personal experience, I have to agree with her. If you're in that spot right now, don't give up. The tide's about to turn!

Writing After Major Losses

After I'd been publishing for a number of years, I had an eight-year period where major personal and professional losses piled on top of each other. During this time, I had four surgeries in thirteen months and took on extra work to pay medical bills. Our teenage adopted child was having severe emotional problems. I went through a divorce, moved twice, remarried, and survived a blended family's three custody battles. Then came the corporate publishing take-over when all eleven of my hardcover books went out of print and my editor lost her job, leaving me an orphaned author.

Block or Burn-Out?

At that point, I could no longer write, and no "Ten Tips for Overcoming Writer's Block" would help me. The common advice was of no use: "Just retype the last page of your previous day's work and you'll be off and running." There wasn't any previous day's work . . . or previous month's either.

I had symptoms of "writer's burn-out." Each symptom is a by-product of prolonged stress. It *can* be treated. Each symptom stifles a writer's creativity in a specific way and needs a specific remedy.

Symptoms

First, my buried feelings refused to come to the surface. I felt like a robot trying to write. My heroine's impassioned speeches were stilted and wooden. Plots I hatched were so worn they were threadbare. Why? Because during a crisis we have to get rigid control over our feelings in order to deal with things. Over many months, "feelings under control" become "frozen feelings." This numbing out spells disaster for writers because we rely on emotions to bring characters and conflict to life.

A second symptom concerns self-image. During stress, self-esteem takes a plunge. To write best, we need to feel good about ourselves. Long-term crises (divorce, child in trouble, job loss) deal heavy blows to even a healthy self-esteem. It leads to increased fears of criticism. How does that affect you as a writer? Even in the best of times, negative reviews and rejected manuscripts are tough to handle. When emotional resources are shot, normal parts of a writer's life become impossible hurdles, and we become fearful of trying any new project.

Third, after prolonged stress, we are often no longer able to unwind. To create, we need a relaxed, "loosened" state of mind. During long-term stress, because of the extraordinary need for tight control of our feelings and behavior, we become rigid and lose our ability to relax that control when the need passes. Always having "everything tightly under control" leaves a writer too rigid to produce a decent rough draft.

Solutions

There are some antidotes to thaw your frozen feelings and restore your confidence. They're simple—but effective.

Tackle your "frozen feelings." Pay attention to yourself, and learn again to identify emotions. You've probably been so centered on others for months that you lost touch with how *you* actually feel. Get re-acquainted with yourself. A simple journal of daily events and the feelings aroused can be very helpful. Sample journal entries: "When John criticized me at lunch I was so furious that my hands shook" or "That meeting with the attorney left me feeling anxious, as if I'd somehow lost his approval." Identify and record those feelings. Try writing out your prayers if that helps you identify feelings.

Work on your self-esteem. Lost self-confidence is sometimes tied to isolation that sets in during periods of long-term stress. We don't feel up to seeing people. It's easy to retreat within our own four walls; writers don't even have to leave the house to go to work. Your office begins to resemble a prison. Even in public, we isolate ourselves from others by "putting on a happy face." To rebuild self-confidence, *break your self-imposed isolation.* Walk to the park, putter around a museum, take an adult education class, go to the movies with a friend, and talk to a counselor. Get out.

Give yourself permission to relax. Let go of trying to control those around you. After living with out-of-control situations, giving up control can seem terrifying. We try to control (and fix and manipulate and caretake) with good intentions. However, giving up the rigid control will probably be necessary if you're to be a productive writer again. Our best work—our most creative—comes from us when we're in those relaxed states of mind. You *can* learn to care without trying to control.

All Healed Now?

Suppose you've come this far. You're now in touch with your feelings, you've come out of isolation, and you're letting other people live their lives while you get on with yours. Does the writing now flow automatically? Unfortunately, no. The final task is to coax your creativity out of hiding. It's not really gone—just merely in hibernation. Often it's only a matter of changing course, being creative in another area of your life for a time. So try another creative outlet. Each person's choice will be different.

For me, flower gardening and quilting did the trick. Just start small (not some big formal garden or king-sized quilt for a wedding). You need a *no-pressure* project. I planted two tiny plots of petunias and impatiens. I stitched individual quilt squares for wall hangings and table coverings. These were small projects that I worked on for ten or fifteen minutes at a time. Slowly, over time, as I stitched and hoed and prayed, my mind's rusty gears started to turn.

It wasn't long before my quilting and gardening time produced more story ideas than flowers or wall decorations, and my burnout was a thing of the past. *Yours can be too.*

Get Your Fear Shot!

We writers fear failure, and we fear success—even though writers don't talk about it much. Wouldn't it be great if you could be inoculated against your writing fears? Get a shot that short-circuits that "fight or flight" response we have to so many things associated with the writing life?

Well, apparently you *can*. The shot takes about thirty to forty seconds to take effect, and if I hadn't tried it myself, I wouldn't have believed it would work.

Bite the Bullet

Many things about the writing life can make us freeze. It might be starting the research on a major project. It might be writing the rough draft of that assignment, needing to pull words out of thin air. Perhaps your "fight or flight" response kicks in when you're hit with revisions—you just don't know where to start!

The "fear inoculation shot" that I read about works for all these things. Since I always have major procrastination problems when working on a rough draft, that's what I decided to test this inoculation on. I can dink around all day getting started, and by 3 p.m. still not have written a single paragraph. So for my shot, I chose the problem of staring at a blank page while needing to write a scene.

Facing Your Foe

This is not your usual "positive imaging" approach. The thirty to forty second "shot" is a mental *rehearsal of you confronting your worst fear.* You put yourself into that scene. (I pictured myself at the computer, staring at the blank screen and the ticking clock as my writing time seeped away.) You shut your eyes and pay very close attention to what's happening in your body. **NOTE:** notice how you react in the first five seconds and write these reactions in a notebook.

- note your physical changes (tension, heart rate, breathing)
- pay attention to the thoughts going around in your head
- listen to what you're telling yourself about the situation

Stick with It

Then, instead of panicking at the fearful reactions you're experiencing—and running for the candy or turning on the TV—*sit with the fear.* Take five or six slow . . . deep . . . breaths and stay focused on the experience you fear. If you stick with it, the author claimed, you will shut off the fight-or-flight response and come into a calmer, more focused level of energy.

Feeling very skeptical (but desperate to get some writing done), I decided to try it. I closed my eyes, pictured the blank screen and the scene I needed to write, and immediately felt tense inside and began breathing faster. I thought *This is really stupid that you have to do this*, and told myself, *You know this will never work.*

I continued to breathe deeply five more times, focusing on that mental blank screen and ticking clock. And I swear, the weirdest thing happened. By the time I'd finished the slow deep breathing, I was (without conscious effort) picturing myself writing and had no trouble beginning! I wrote for forty-five minutes and got some good writing completed. Later, after answering some email, I decided to try it again. I took another forty-second fear shot and wrote another hour!

Multi-Purpose Shot

I was so intrigued by these results that I applied the "fear shot" to other writing fears. One of these is a fear of success. This may sound silly, but "fear of success" can also be a reason for procrastinating with your writing and submitting.

Beyond Publication

What form can "fear of success" take? I can think of several possibilities, based on questions I am asked:

Fear of exposure: My parents/siblings/spouse will read what I really think about them.

Post publication panic: I'm scared of the idea of marketing (e.g., giving speeches and doing book signings).
Fear of being a "one-shot wonder": People will expect me to write another—even better—book.
Fear of bad reviews: My peers will see them.
Fear of no reviews: My book will be totally ignored.
Fear of poor sales: I'll never get a second chance with a publisher.
Fearing reality: Getting published may not give my life meaning, save my marriage, or resurrect my self-esteem.

The fear shot idea can be applied to each of those very real fears. But what if our fears are irrational and not based on truth?

Reframing Fear

We all interpret our emotions. As Beth Jacobs says in *Writing for Emotional Balance*, an emotion is first a physical response, the stimulation of a pathway of nerve cells in the brain (e.g., a specific pathway has been identified for the feeling of anxiety, which activates certain physical responses). You then interpret—you make decisions about—the physical symptoms and the stimulus that caused the anxious reaction.

Many of our writing fears are irrational and we interpret the fear signals incorrectly. (The blank page can't really hurt me, so there is no rational reason to fear it.) Many of a writer's fears aren't real. They're False Evidence Appearing Real. We take "evidence" like a rejection, and we birth a host of fears: *I'm afraid I'll never be published, I'm afraid the economy is too weak for me to succeed, I'm afraid I'm wasting my time writing, I'm afraid I'm too young/old to write.* Or we look at our other past failures and conclude, *I'll never succeed at writing either.*

Re-frame and Move On

Most often, our writing fears have no more substance than my grandson's deathly fear of thunder. Fear makes a lot of noise, but it's just noise. So decide to interpret circumstances a different way—one that is just as plausible—and watch the fear evaporate.

Got a rejection? It doesn't mean your writing is poor. It's just as likely that the reason is the economy, or maybe the magazine already accepted a similar piece. Rejections in the past are no predictor of future success either. It's much like Edison's response when someone asked him how it felt to fail to invent the light bulb 1000+ times. He claimed that none of those efforts were failures. He had been successful at finding more than 1000 things that didn't work. He always expected the next try might be the one to succeed. Eventually, it was.

> When your negative writing circumstances could be interpreted in a more positive light, do that for yourself. You'll get rid of irrational fear, you'll free up your creativity again (which thrives on hope, not pessimism), and you'll be prepared for a writing career that can last for decades. *Reframing fear is not an optional skill.* It's a must-have for your writing survival.

If re-framing your fear doesn't eliminate it, then get in line for your fear shot! Do whatever you need to do. There *are* ways to deal with your fears—and eliminate them!

Family Matters

Setting Boundaries So You Can Write

Juggling writing and a family can be a delicate balancing act sometimes! If you tend to be a people pleaser—if the word "no" isn't in your vocabulary—you'll find making time to write especially hard. It's difficult when wistful family members stand there looking so, well, *needy*. You'll have to give yourself permission to set a few boundaries with family, friends, and co-workers—and then learn how to enforce those boundaries in a kind—but firm—manner.

Boundary? What's That?

Once I cleaned and cooked all day Saturday for guests who never showed up and didn't call to explain until the next day that their plans had changed. I could have spent that day writing. I fumed, but did nothing about it. Another time I showed up for a lunch meeting on time, but a person critical to the planning was an hour late. The (unnecessary) lateness then made me miss an event I had been looking forward to for weeks. Judging from the acid in my stomach and tension in my neck, it was time to set some limits.

Trust Yourself

Being an approval junkie, I used to cringe at setting boundaries. (e.g., "If you aren't here by 11:30, we'll have to leave without you.") Claiming sufficient writing time and energy has been a thirty-year learning experience. Learning to say "no" and learning to claim writing time is harder for some than others.

Setting boundaries so that we can write is about learning to take care of ourselves as writers, no matter where we go or who we're with. Boundaries emerge from deep decisions about what we believe we deserve (and don't deserve). The ability to set boundaries increases as we get it through our thick skulls that what we want and need as writers (time, solitude, new experiences) is vitally important. Boundaries emerge as we learn to value, trust, and listen to the writer within.

Recognize Boundary Issues

This isn't as easy as it sounds. One writer has been writing for six years and still finds it a struggle. "I'm good at setting boundaries with my friends and family once I realize something is hurting me or making me angry; it still takes forever, though, to recognize when something bothers me."

We're all good at stuffing our feelings and staying busy enough to ignore them, but boundary issues don't stay confined to our minds. As psychologist Harriet Lerner says, "We need to listen to our bodies to know where our boundaries are."

For a variety of reasons, we may be adept at ignoring the knot in the stomach, the headache, the cramped neck, the sadness that occurs when people invade and take over our time, space and energy. The next time you feel this way, don't automatically reach for the Excedrin® or Pepcid AC®; consider instead whether it's a physical reaction to boundary violations.

Anger, rage, complaining, and whining are clues to boundaries we need to set. Other clues might include feeling threatened or suffocated when around certain people. Listen closely to yourself.

Set Necessary Boundaries

Even after recognizing the anger and hurt when your boundaries have been trampled, it can be difficult to think clearly about the situation and decide what to do. I have found journaling a big help at such times.

Writing brings clarity, which is no surprise to most writers! Describe the incident in your journal. Write how you feel about it. Is it related to your writing? Is it a pattern with this person? What do you need to do? Write out what you might say. Practice until you can say it firmly, but with kindness. If you're still angry when you finish, perhaps a letter setting the boundary would be better than a face-to-face confrontation.

Set limits clearly, using as few words as possible. Avoid justifying, rationalizing, or apologizing. Offer a brief explanation, if that would help, but don't get trapped into being defensive. ("I know you want to have company again this weekend, but I really need some down time, with no company.") If they insist (however nicely) on inviting people over, just say, "That's fine. I know our needs are different. I'll plan to spend the day up at the lake (or at the library, or wherever) to unwind and write." Smile! End of discussion!

> By the way, don't try to set boundaries with people while simultaneously fixing their upset feelings. *It can't be done.* Their feelings and reactions to your boundary will probably be negative, but they are responsible for those feelings, not you.

Speaking up and setting boundaries is one thing. Enforcing limits is quite another.

Enforce Boundaries

I should mention that some people will be perfectly happy to respect your boundaries. They've simply been unaware that their actions cause you any distress. We are very good at hiding our frustration, by saying "Oh, it's okay," when our writing time is interrupted for the umpteenth time. These people will gladly make changes when we speak up.

On the other hand, people who have been able to control and use us will react more negatively. There's an old saying: "People don't respect people they can use. People use people they can use, and respect people they can't use." Users may get angry with you for setting a boundary, especially if it forces them to take more responsibility for themselves. That's okay.

Be aware of one thing however: *It does no good to set a boundary until you're ready to enforce it.* So convince *yourself* first. Once you know deep down what your limits are, what your true needs are, it won't be difficult to convince others. Haven't you noticed that people tend to have a sixth sense about when you've truly reached your limit?

This Is Only a Test!

You will be tested when you set boundaries. *Plan on it.* They might be little tests: your toddler curls up and sucks her thumb when you sit down to write. They might be big tests: your wife or husband threatens to "find someone else who's agreeable like you used to be."

Sometimes you have to get mad (and noisy!) to set boundaries, but you don't have to stay mad to enforce them. If you're prone to "people pleasing" and approval seeking, however, demons will come out to torment you for a while when you set boundaries, threatening you with losses both real and imaginary. Just stay calm—and quiet. Be confident and go on about your business. If you can do this, their protests will die down fairly quickly.

Do be prepared to follow through on any consequences you've mentioned or boundaries you've set. If your boundary is that you will write undisturbed in your bedroom from 3-4 p.m., yet you allow your children to interrupt while you whine about it, it's not a boundary yet. Our boundaries must match our behavior. Just remember, boundaries aren't made to control others' behavior, just our own. The kids may keep trying to interrupt; you may have to lock your bedroom door and ignore the screams.

Carve Out the Time
Often we writers are given tips for carving writing time out of our busy lives. We look for hidden pockets of time to write. We set aside time alone to think, to do research, to journal. *All the planning in the world, however, won't do a bit of good unless you set and enforce boundaries* with those who (for whatever reasons) feel they own all your time.

Setting and enforcing boundaries is difficult at first, but the sense of freedom they bring—as well as time to pursue your writing dream—makes it well worthwhile.

Creativity and Noise: Do They Mix?

What conditions do you need in order to write?

Are you an introvert who thrives on silence and solitude, but your muse goes into hiding when people and noise invade your space? Or are you someone who prefers to write in a three-ring circus? You can write in the family room, amidst video games and kids arguing, or in airport waiting rooms with TVs blaring and people yelling on cell phones.

What's Your Ideal Writing Environment?

Some writers can't write when it gets too quiet and they feel isolated from the family fun. Other writers freeze up if anyone else is even in the house, much less the same room. Some moms write while soothing fussy babies, stopping every half hour because they are potty training a toddler too. (Those were my early writing days.)

My ideal writing environment is what I have most days now. My kids are grown, so there are no babies crying, no teens on cell phones, no stereos blasting. I no longer live beneath horribly noisy apartment neighbors. We are on a quiet street, and our house borders a woodsy greenbelt area. After several years of this, I wonder if I've totally lost the ability to write in less-than-ideal environments.

I have several friends who write in coffee shops, and that has always been my secret ideal image of a writer. But I hate coffee, and I can't write with noise and commotion (and a glass case of desserts) to distract me. Unless it's a nonfiction project, I can't write in restaurants.

> Whatever type of ideal writing environment you prefer is fine. Get to know yourself. Find out the conditions that help you thrive as a writer. Then take steps to approximate that environment as much as you can.

Can You Create Your Ideal Spot?

Suppose you're a young mom who has trouble writing with noise and commotion. What can you do to bring elements of peace into your writing place? I recall getting all four babies/toddlers/preschoolers down for naps at the same time in order to have the quiet solitude I needed to do the actual writing. I used play times with the kids (or times cooking or folding diapers) to pre-think my plot, dialogue, and character problems.

During the teen years, I invested in some first class ear plugs and a white noise machine for my office. I used them again when I lived in a very noisy apartment complex. You can find the machines at WalMart and also in most baby departments. If noise bothers you, do what you can to eliminate or muffle much of it. Otherwise, you'll use up half your writing energy just trying to blot out disturbing racket.

Get out a notebook or open a computer file and journal about the following:

- What is your IDEAL writing environment?
- What is your REAL writing environment?
- What can you do to bring elements of the IDEAL into your REAL life?

Sometimes the *simplest* things can make the biggest difference!

Hats Off to Mom Writers!

Mom writers are a special breed, and my hat goes off to you. (All moms are special, but *writer* moms require a whole extra skill set!)

I started writing when my children were babies and toddlers, but I haven't been in that life stage for a long time. However, I babysit grandkids a lot. The nine days my grandkids (ages three and six then) stayed with us during spring break were a great reminder. That week (which is different than babysitting a few hours) brought back quickly the challenges of combining children and writing—both finding *time* and finding *energy*.

It also reminded me of the very real blessing it is to have children around on a daily basis when you write for children. As Katherine Paterson once said:

> *"As I look back on what I have written, I can see that the very persons who have taken away my time are those who have given me something to say."*

I love that quote. Every mom writer knows that to be true.

Hands-On Research
When my grandkids stayed with us for a week, I was writing a middle-grade novel that included a kindergarten boy. Until their visit the character was pretty flat—one of those story people who just lie there on the page. I couldn't seem to get the dialogue quite right, and the humor went over like a lead balloon.

After their visit, though, the problem was a thing of the past. I collected a small notebook of ideas gleaned from watching the kids all week—at the park, playing dress-up, investigating birds and bugs, and turning cardboard boxes into boats and sleds. Then I could populate my stories with the actions and dialogue of *real* kids.

Help for Mamas

Mixing babies and bylines can be a real challenge though. Years ago, I relied heavily on a book that is now out of print. However, a friend recommended a book for writer/moms called *Writer Mama: How to Raise a Writing Career Alongside Your Kids* by Christina Katz. Judging by the large number of five-star reviews on Amazon, it could be just what the doctor ordered if you're balancing kids and writing career.

Also there are many blogs and websites especially for moms who write. Google search terms like "mom writers" and "mom writer blogs" to find the most helpful ones. With the help of the Internet, you can now find support from other mom writers without ever leaving home.

Can You Have It Both Ways?

If you have a family—whether it's preschoolers and toddlers like I had when I started writing, or grandkids like I have now—it's something you have to consider when trying to write. It's a balancing act, especially if your family comes first in your heart, as mine does.

It's no good putting the writing before your family and then living in guilt. The guilt will short circuit your writing and create a solid writer's block. So, how can you make more time to write without short-changing your family? It's a juggling act!

Tight Rope Balancing Act

In the second *Glimmer Train Guide to Writing Fiction*, the volume called *Inspiration and Discipline*, an interesting point was made. A mother/writer was asked about balancing family and writing.

In part, she made this observation:

> *"It's very hard. There's no way of glossing it over. It's very, very difficult. At this point, my children are grown, but still they're—of course—more important than my work. And that's how it is . . . I sometimes think back through history: Were there any great women writers with children? I've been unable to find any. Of course, the way history is written, we*

don't know . . . but those whom we know didn't have children and families."

I had never thought about that, but my favorite female writers (Jane Austen, Louisa May Alcott, the Brontés, and others) *were* single women without children.

Can You Be Both Parent and Writer?

What do you think is the reason behind that fact? Is it merely the time needed to raise a family, preventing you giving enough time to the writing? Or is it that both writing and raising children take the same kind of dedication, love, focus, and sheer energy?

Can babies and bylines mix? Or if you try to do both, do both suffer?

I don't personally think either has to *suffer*, although there are only 24 hours in anyone's day. You probably can't be as prolific while raising five kids! You may end up writing five great young adult books instead of ten, but they can still be awesome, award-winning books.

Or maybe you'll be just as prolific, but your house won't be as white-glove clean as your mother-in-law's. Or you'll oversee the school's Christmas party instead of volunteering as room mother all year long. There are changes you can make—things you can give up—that won't affect either the quality of your writing or the quality of your parenting. It doesn't have to be an either/or.

> ### It's *Your* Life
> The balance you decide on is a choice only you can make, but once it's made, *move ahead without guilt*. No one else can live your life, and outsiders don't get to vote. People may be free with their opinions ("You'd be better off growing vegetables," or "You need to get a real job.") but you can learn to ignore them. Or make them the villains in your next book!

Household Have-To's

Families: what would we do without them?

Writers want to keep up with their homes and families, yet also write, but there just doesn't seem to be enough time. Maintaining our homes (even if we have no Martha Stewart aspirations) and keeping our families fed and clothed can consume so much time that the would-be writer finally throws up her hands and shelves her writing dreams for "later," when there will be more time.

Warning! "Later" won't come. Sad, but definitely true. There is only *now*, and without making some household changes, there won't *ever* be time to write. As seasons come and go, your chores and responsibilities will change, but the time to write won't magically materialize. You have to make it appear.

Planned Procrastination

Like many new writers, I didn't think I could sit down at the keyboard unless the dishes and laundry were done, the carpet vacuumed, and the children happily entertained with Play-Doh®. I had tried writing before polishing off these household chores, but the anxiety and guilt got the better of me. And, of course, since I felt guilty, I must be doing something wrong. Right?

So I returned to my "work now, play later" philosophy, washing dishes during my prime creative time and writing late in the day when I had no energy left. Not until years later, when I realized writing was also work, did a paradigm shift occurred. Then I finally put household chores in their place.

Elaine Fantle Shimberg, author of *Write Where You Live*, says,

"If you can put household chores in their proper place—something that must be done eventually—you can make and stick to a writing schedule that works for you. Do what needs to be done as it needs to be done, then do it as efficiently and effectively as it needs to be done and nothing more." (Unless your mother's coming to visit.) She called it "planned procrastination."

Does It Have To Be Done?

How do you decide what has to be done and what doesn't? It's a personal decision, but look critically at how you spend your time. Are you working around the house doing things no one ever notices (rearranging the photos, painting daisies on your flower pots, alphabetizing books by author)? Then stop it. In most families, spouses and children notice when there's no food to eat, no clean clothes to wear, and you're out of shampoo. Pretty much everything else is optional.

So decide what is critical to you, then stop doing everything else. Personally, I need the house picked up before I can work, but dishes in the sink can wait. You may be the opposite. *Experiment.* Try leaving certain jobs undone while you write—or undone altogether—and see what really bothers you and what doesn't. Perhaps you were raised to mop the kitchen floor every Saturday, so you've done it for years. You may discover once a month suits you fine, with mini wipe-ups between times.

Remember the purpose of the experiment: *time saved is time you can spend writing.*

Organize!

If you organize your household have-to's, you'll find more time to write. Do you run errands several times per week and wander around stores trying to remember what you need? Then combine your trips into one morning, make lists before you leave home, map out an efficient route, and easily save yourself several hours per week.

If you have a choice, run those errands in off-peak times. Save at least an hour each week by not visiting banks, laundromats, pharmacies, post offices, and grocery stores in the evenings, on weekends, or just before closing time.

Consider boxing up or throwing away all your clutter gathering dust. Clear off desks, kitchen counter tops, bathroom counters and cabinets, coffee tables, and dressers. Cleared surfaces are faster to dust and make you feel in control of your home. File or trash the clipped recipes, old medicines, and past issues of anything. Put away appliances you rarely use, like the bread maker, juicer, blender, and toaster oven. Make space to work. *Then appropriate that saved time to write.*

Supper Time!
Food shopping, preparation and cleanup are NOT one of the household have-to's you'll be allowed to skip. So streamline and enlist help. Put a grocery list on the refrigerator and insist that everyone add requests to the list in writing. (No more of this "Hey, Mom! We're out of . . .") If it's not on the list, you don't buy it. Train family members to add items to the list when they use the last of it.

As soon as your kids have drivers' licenses, make grocery shopping (with the list) one of their chores. (It pays off! My oldest daughter met her future husband this way. He was her carryout boy for a year before he actually carried her off.)

Streamline your cooking too. If your children are too small to help, then fix double or triple portions when you cook, and freeze a meal or two. Why spend two one-hour periods cooking two meals of meatballs, when you can cook that amount in one hour, freeze a meal, and use that saved hour for writing?

If your children are ten or older, they can take turns cooking and cleaning up afterwards. My children, from age ten on, were assigned one night per week to cook and also do dishes. (That way the sloppy cooks had to clean up their own messes afterwards.) There are great kids' cookbooks, and my children enjoyed trying new things. If they wanted to cook something special, they added those items to the grocery list.

After you decide which chores really need doing, schedule those tasks according to your inner clock. Don't waste your most alert hours sweeping floors and washing dishes. If you're mentally sharp in the mornings, write first. If you're brain dead upon awakening, clean toilets then—and write late at night when your muse comes out of hiding. I have found, after writing a couple hours, that washing dishes or sorting laundry makes a good break—and is *unfun* enough to prod me back quickly to the keyboard!

You own your house. Don't let it—and its tasks—own you. Take a hard look at your current household have-to's, and see where you can cut or streamline. Make the changes. Then spend that "found" time writing instead.

We All Live Here

Anyone who lives under your roof should be helping with chores. Even the youngest child can pick up toys. Elementary children can make and change their beds, take out garbage, do dishes, vacuum, and fold laundry. Older children and teens can grocery shop, scoop snow, wash cars, and mow the lawn as well. Rotate the chores as much as possible. No one enjoys cleaning bathrooms, so make everyone take a turn. "Many hands make light work," my grandma always said. And she was right.

Writers: Always Working

If you're a plumber hired to unclog my drain, but I catch you sitting and looking out the window, I can, in all fairness, say you're not working. If you're my cleaning lady, but I catch you rocking in a chair staring into space, I can say justly that you're not working.

What about writers? *Not so easy to tell!*

Thinking vs. Writing

According to Wallace Stevens, "It is not always easy to tell the difference between thinking and looking out the window." It's also not always easy to tell the difference between a writer thinking and going for a walk; between thinking and washing dishes; between thinking and daydreaming; and between thinking and grazing in the fridge.

Why is this true? Because *lots of thinking precedes writing.*

Purposes of Thinking

For fiction writers, thinking about characters, getting to know them, listening to their voices—all this happens in the head while "thinking." Plot twists and turns give birth while "thinking"—and woe unto the writer who skips thinking and writes the first thing that comes into his head.

Although all this pre-thinking or preparation stage is critical, that isn't all the thinking you'll have to do. Even while working on revisions, you'll find yourself thinking and staring out the window, thinking and walking, thinking and grazing. *You* understand that "I'm thinking" means "so please don't interrupt." Chances are, your family won't. Instead they will walk into the room where you're "thinking-writing" and say, "Oh good, you're not doing anything. Can you hold the ladder for me?"

Thinking in Disguise

That's why I prefer to do my thinking in private if I can. Otherwise it just seems to invite interruptions, often at a critical moment when I've just about figured out my theme or where the climax scene needs to go.

If I'm home alone, that's no problem. If it's in the evening, though, or on a weekend, I weed flowers or fold a load of laundry or wash dishes when I need to think something through. Nobody bothers you when doing chores—they might get roped into helping.

> **Reap the Rewards**
> Contrary to the life of a plumber or housekeeper, a lot of the writer's real work happens when she's looking out the window. Sometimes my clearest thoughts, my best insights for how to fix things, come when I'm not thinking about the piece of writing at all. Give yourself enough of this "mindless" time, and you'll be amazed what bubbles up to your conscious mind.

Despite the heckling you may receive, during this thinking time know that you're a writer at work. Keep on thinking. The pay-off will be huge.

Just Busy—or Crazy Busy?

A writer friend of mine and I had been talking about New Year's goals for two months when she sent me this excerpt from a newsletter.

Is This You?
In part, it said, *"You're doing well, you're successful, and you enjoy life, but do you feel frustrated at how hard you have to struggle to keep up with all your commitments, opportunities, deadlines, and messages? Do you keep thinking there must be a better way?"*

Then the author, Dr. Edward Hallowell, said something that SHOCKED me.

He said such a person should feel *proud for being crazy-busy, over-booked, and about to snap.* He said it meant that this person had a lot of interests, high curiosity, and lots of enthusiasm. It was the sign of a responsible and daring person.

Oh Really?
Hmmm . . . maybe there *are* crazy-busy people like that. Not me though!

Sure, I'd love to think that those nutty periods in my life meant I was daring and enthusiastic. Unfortunately, I'm afraid that when my life is "crazy busy," it's more likely to be that I couldn't say "no" to yet another commitment (or to solving someone else's self-created problem). Caretakers—whether by choice or dysfunction—are some of the craziest-busiest people I've known.

Of course, whether your life is crazy-busy because you're such an enthusiastic go-getter or because you can't seem to set priorities and stick to them, the result is really the same: inner and outer chaos, overload, and little time to concentrate and write.

Are You in Danger?
All this crazy busy-ness brings a host of problems with it. What danger signs of overload (results of a crazy-busy life) should you look out for?

- irritability
- impaired performance
- fatigue
- forgetfulness
- loss of sense of humor
- inability to tolerate interruptions or conflict
- loss of mental flexibility
- inability to listen to others
- loss of hope
- tendency to blame others
- musculoskeletal aches and pains
- headaches
- loss of focus and concentration

If you identify with many of those symptoms, read on—and ask yourself some tough questions.

Solutions?
The author said that most crazy-busy people who get behind and feel pressured and stressed tend to make a big mistake. They work even harder. They put their heads down, nose to the grindstone, and determine to stop complaining and work till they drop.

He likened it to pushing down hard on the accelerator when your car is mired in mud. Messy, and it really doesn't get you anywhere, so you shouldn't just "work harder." For the most part, I agree. However, there will be those times—when you have a child who is in the hospital, or some other true emergency—when working harder is necessary. You just do it.

Each person is different, and the reasons we become crazy-busy are different. However, no matter what the reasons are, the real question is this:

Can You Keep It Up? Really?

Do you ever find yourself saying things like:

- "I just can't do this anymore."
- "If I have to keep this schedule one more year, it will kill me."
- "I feel like I'm treading water and going under."

When I hear these comments from writers and students, it makes me want to ask each one: *Are you living a sustainable life?*

A Crazy Pace

Too many of us are living crazy-busy lives. We have no margins anywhere anymore. There are no gaps between the end of one activity and the beginning of another one. When your activities overlap with no "down time" in between, your stress goes up and your creativity goes down.

And when you try to cram one more thing—writing—into an already crazy-busy life, it rarely works. Writing requires at least a decent amount of relaxed, quiet thinking time. Maybe you combine that solitude with walking (or pushing a stroller), but you need *some*.

Build In Some Margins

Are *YOU* living a sustainable life? Or, if you continue at your current pace, will it eventually ruin your health? Without making changes, you may never be able to fit in the writing time you dream of.

If your current life isn't sustainable over the long haul, take *out* some activities—then build *in* some margins of down time. I encourage you to give your schedule some serious thought. Take charge of it instead of letting outside forces take charge of *you*.

A Parent's Writing Schedule

When my children were small—and even as they grew older—I struggled to find a writing schedule that worked most days of the week. After much trial and error, I would hit upon a schedule that allowed me to write nearly two hours per day. Bliss!

Not for Long

That "bliss" lasted a very short time usually—until I once again had morning sickness, or someone was teething, or my husband switched to working nights, or someone started school, or someone else went out for three extra-curricular activities, and we lived in the car after school and weekends.

> It was many years before I realized there is no *one right way* to schedule my writing. The "right way" (by my own definition) is simply the schedule that allows me to get some writing done on a regular basis.

Flexibility Is the Name of the Game

How can you schedule your writing? Let me count the ways:

First, be an early morning writer. Even if you're not naturally a morning person, you can train yourself to be one. It was never my natural inclination, but today I can't imagine sleeping in, even if I tried. There are so many pluses for writing early: the house is quieter, the phone is quieter, no one comes to the door, it's not time to cook or run errands, and you can still parent or go to your day job at the normal time. Morning is a fresher time to write for most people. The added bonus is that once it's done, it's done for the day! You don't have to keep trying to squeeze it in somewhere.

Second, be a night-time writer. If your biological clock says you're an owl, and there's no changing it, then write after hours. It's also quiet on the tail end of the day. The kids are asleep, the spouse is watching TV or reading, the phone is quieter, no one rings the doorbell, and you're finished with cooking and running errands and your day job. Actively plan to finish up necessary chores (homework checking, making school lunches) before your set time for writing—and then *write*.

Third, be an office writer. If you have any kind of day job, chances are that depriving yourself of morning sleep won't work. And you may be too drained from your job at night to do much writing. So learn to write a bit before work (if you can get there early), during lunch or scheduled breaks, and then stay at your desk (or in your parked car with your laptop) after work for half an hour. If you have a private office—or just a quiet place before others show up for work—consider getting there early with your writing materials and/or staying a bit late after others go home.

Fourth, be a nose-to-the-grindstone writer. Suppose for whatever reasons, you can't write much at all during the week. You have newborn triplets and take care of your parents as well, run a home daycare, and are the PTA chairman. You hate to write in short spurts, but given the opportunity, you *can* hunker down and write for eight hours without coming up for air. If that's your style, make your schedule around that. Have your spouse or a babysitter do a day of child care for you on weekends and hole up at the library (or hide in the attic) for the day.

Fifth, be a mini-block writer. This is how I wrote for at least two years. Ten minutes at a time. Occasionally fifteen. I grabbed bits and pieces when I could. I wrote on the typewriter sometimes, or on a pad of paper in my purse in the doctor's waiting room, or scribbled on a tablet while sitting in bleachers waiting for an event to start. I could write a whole page in fifteen minutes if I took time to think it through before I sat down at the keyboard. It adds up. I wrote my first five middle-grade novels this way.

Where There's a Will . . .
If you want to write badly enough, you'll find a way. Just remember that even when you find the perfect schedule, it's only perfect for right *now*. As circumstances change, often our writing schedules have to change. Experiment with all the different types of schedules and see which ones work best for you, given the circumstances you're presently living with.

Just remember that you have *choices*—but quitting isn't one of them!

Writing Through Relationship Struggles

Do these scenarios sound at all familiar?

- You're writing your first picture book, but your husband is jealous of your time at the computer and won't speak to you at supper. (I know this sounds childish, but it happens fairly often.)
- Your wife reads your book and asks you what makes you think you're a writer. (This actually happened, but these struggles are not gender-specific.)
- You're struggling to write, but your recent marital separation has left you too depressed and exhausted to concentrate.
- Your wife gained fifty pounds to protest how much time you spend writing. (Yes, this actually happened to a writer friend—his wife told him what she planned to do and then did it.)

How to Keep Writing

Many talented writers lose confidence and lay aside their writing dreams because of marital and relationship problems. THIS ISN'T NECESSARY. However, it does require you to fall back and regroup when you have an unsupportive spouse, whether this person is just mildly irritated with you or has distanced to the point of separation.

What can you do if you find yourself in any of these situations?

Develop faith in yourself. Rather than looking for outside support, look inside. The decision to write is made—and carried out—alone. Then write daily, even if just a journal entry. Nothing—no matter how long you write or how much you are published—builds faith faster that you're a *real writer* than the physical act of writing every day.

Create a support system. Perhaps you can join or form a writers' group that can offer you encouragement. Attend writers' conferences to hear inspirational speakers. Clip or photocopy encouraging articles from *The Writer* and *Writer's Digest* to re-read when needed. (I have a six-inch thick file of such articles.) Pray frequently.

Change your writing time. When I worked at a dental office during my separation (for added income), I wrote for an hour before work and during my lunch hour, a totally different writing schedule for me. Surprisingly, the break in routine was effective.

Change your surroundings. Our surroundings hold memories. And when they're bad memories, they stifle our creativity. So change your place of writing. Work in the library or another room in the house—a place not associated with painful events.

Just write. Writing won't necessarily banish depression, but depression doesn't have to banish the writing either. Don't wait until you feel happy to write. *Just keep writing*. Don't edit at this point—nothing sounds good when you're depressed. Write instead. Journal. Write out your prayers if praying is difficult at this time.

(A resource you may find helpful is *Writing for Emotional Balance: A Guided Journal to Help You Manage Overwhelming Emotions* by Beth Jacobs.)

> Relationship struggles of one kind or another happen to most people eventually. It doesn't have to mean the end of your writing. Take specific planned steps to keep putting one writing foot in front of the other.
>
> You want to have a career left when the dust settles—and you *can*.

Combining Babies, Bylines, and School-Age Children

I started writing when I had an infant, a two-year-old, and a pre-schooler. I wrote throughout their school years, their teen years, their college/adult years, and now have come full circle when I babysit grandkids.

The (survival) skills you need to both write and parent change with each stage of your children's lives. Sometimes your biggest need is time or energy. Other times your biggest need is keeping your sanity! This chapter (plus the following chapter "Writing During the Teen and Early Adult Years") will give you practical ways to combine writing and parenting throughout these life stages.

Just as beneficial, I hope I can show you some ways that your kids (and later, grandchildren) can be your best sources of material. Let's start at the very beginning.

Writing with Infants and Small Children

When raising babies and small children, FINDING TIME to write is the toughest ask. Try these ideas:

- **Jot down story and article ideas when you're forced to sit**—in waiting rooms, while nursing the baby, etc.

- **Pre-write.** Think through your plot lines, article openings, and titles while doing non-think activities like cooking supper and vacuuming. You don't have time to waste at the keyboard. You may only have ten minutes, so be ready to write when you get to the computer.

- **Outline.** When you sit down to write, you'll know exactly where you are if you've written a clear outline; you won't waste time getting started.

- **Keep writing supplies organized, in one spot, out of little ones' reach.** For years I wrote in a small closet painted orange with a door on it for this reason. I didn't care that it was too tiny to turn around in. It was mine, and my materials stayed put!

- **Hire a sitter or barter with a friend to trade babysitting.** I never did this, but I know others have. Use these uninterrupted blocks of time for serious writing. Save other miscellaneous writing chores for those tiny segments of free time.

Turn Childhood Experiences into Salable Manuscripts

One such experience with my small children became an article for *Farm Woman* (later called *Country Woman*) entitled "Treasure This Day," which was reprinted in *Catholic Digest*. It was a simple article about the joys and frustrations of gardening with a baby, a toddler, and preschooler in tow.

Another book, *For Every Joy That Passes*, has a mother in it who runs a daycare in her home; many of my baby and toddler experiences went in there.

My published stories, articles, and books based almost directly on my kids would take pages to list. Just be aware that your children—especially when you write for the juvenile market—are one of your best research sources.

Writing and School-Age Kids

There are challenges galore when writing with newborns and babies in the house. At that stage, we usually daydream of that magical day when the kids will be in school and we'll have all those uninterrupted hours to write.

Yes, it is *easier* to write when kids are older, but not necessarily *easy*. You still need ways to be there for your family while making time for quality writing.

Wearing So Many Hats

Life is hectic at this time, with chauffeuring kids to baseball and ballet. You may also work full- or part-time outside the home. More demands are made on your evenings and weekends. At this stage, the key is to be **flexible** and **disciplined**.

- **Write wherever/whenever you can.** I finished an entire novel by writing in the orthodontist's waiting room, bleachers during basketball practice, and the doctor's office while my daughter got her weekly allergy shots.

- **If you work outside the home**, write on the bus if you commute. Use a voice activated tape recorder if you have to drive. Write during your lunch hour. When I worked as a receptionist I took my laptop to work with me and wrote during my lunch hour—and got a surprising amount written. And there's always pen and paper.

- **Go to the library** to write some evenings or weekends. Grab a few hours of peace and quiet there. (I still do that—to make myself stay off the Internet and work!) If you can concentrate in a book store or coffee shop, take your writing there for a couple hours.

- **Limit TV, volunteering, and lunches out** if your days are free while your children are in school. You must CHOOSE writing and choose it first whenever possible, before other activities. When helping at your kids' schools, volunteer for ONE activity at the beginning of the school year (e.g., help with the Christmas party) instead of becoming room mother or some job that takes many hours per month. (Remember: more than one school-age child multiplies the requests for volunteering.)

- **When working at home, use an answering machine and voice mail.** Kids learn to remember their own homework and lunches if you're no longer available to run forgotten items to school.

Turn Experiences into Manuscripts

Much of my early publishing success came directly from parenting school-age kids. I wrote articles like "Telephone Safety" for *Jack and Jill*. I also wrote novels like *The Haunting of Cabin 13* (children's choice award winner) after camping with my school-age kids in Backbone State Park in Iowa.

My children helped me be a better writer—and writing daily helped me be a better (happier) mom!

> Parenting babies and school-age children doesn't have to mean choosing between your family and your writing. Try combining them instead. These age groups provide you with rich material. Make flexibility your watch word, and you'll be able to juggle both.

Writing During the Teen and Early Adult Years

Your writing career has survived infancy, toddlers, and school age children. You've learned to be flexible. That's good. Next come the teen years, and then the years when your children are in their twenties and thirties. Each age group comes with its own special challenges for the determined writer!

Surviving and Thriving with Teens

The main challenge with writing during the teen years is keeping (and constantly regaining) your sanity! Even normally active teens can leave a parent hyper, worried, deaf, and frustrated: *not* a state conducive to your best writing. Teens in ongoing trouble can just about finish you off.

Over the years, I discovered some helpful tips for writing with teens in the house . . .

- **Use ear plugs.** Try those soft foam ones, like miniature marshmallows. Ear plugs block out stereos, giggling girls, phones ringing, and TV.

- **Adjust your schedule—because the kids won't/can't adjust theirs.** On weekends I waited up to ensure that each child got home safely from part-time jobs and dates. I used to doze by the TV and then was too tired to write in the morning, which I resented. So, despite the difficulty making the switch, I started writing from ten to midnight on weekends. Then I would sleep late the next morning without guilt.

- **Try some free-flowing ten-minute writing exercises** during a teenager's *roughest* times (drug problems, pregnancies, school problems). These issues can come close to derailing an author's ability to write. The problems might last for months—or years—and can be a source of major writer's block. If this is your situation, throughout the day journal to unblock, writing about whatever you're feeling.

- **Just keep writing—anything.** Keep the words flowing during these high-stress times so your ability to write is intact when the crisis finally passes.

Some of those ten-minute segments may later provide you with story/article ideas for teens or parents. Perhaps, with teens underfoot, you'll write a nonfiction book for parents like my favorite self-help title: *Get Out of My Life, But First Could You Drive Me and Cheryl to the Mall?*

Is there any doubt that this author merged raising kids with his writing?

Mixing Writing and Adult Children

Just when your days (or evenings and weekends) are blissfully free to write, your college-age children are home for the summer. They turn your precise schedule upside down. They also provide such a temptation to sit and chat and go shopping or out for lunch. Or maybe your adult child moves back home, perhaps with small children.

This "temporary" situation with an adult child may extend for months—even years.

I'm Glad You're Here, But . . .

Just as in all other stages of child-raising, this "adult child" stage requires a writer to be very flexible. (This *doesn't* mean you give up your writing.) Perhaps more than any other age, this stage requires diplomacy. The grown children visitors in your home will see themselves as adults (with adult privileges), but not always with adult responsibilities. They may expect to come and go as they please, have friends in at all hours—and yet not buy any groceries or help clean house or do their own laundry.

Sit down and have a talk with your grown children before they come home. Discuss what rules you still need to have followed. (It *is* your house! Remember that.) Talk about things like division of labor and chores (or you'll be too busy to find time to write). Talk about noise levels, both day and evening (or the pounding drum practice will keep you from writing).

> As a writer who works at home, you have some special needs. The flexibility is needed so you can find alternate ways to meet those needs.

Here are some practical ideas that writers with adult children at home have used to keep writing:

- **Don't abandon your schedule!** These people aren't company or house guests. For the time being, they are simply living with you. Your life doesn't need to revolve around them. *Keep to your schedule.*

- **Deal with possible interruptions ahead of time.** Say something like this to them: "I start work early, but help yourselves to the eggs and juice in the fridge." Don't wait on them hand and foot. Resist the urge to clean up their messes in the kitchen and living room until your writing time is finished.

- **If your writing room is needed for sleeping space, turn a corner of your bedroom into a temporary study.** Have a place where you can close the door and write. Put up a sign if you need to.

- **Turn this time into productive writing by taking advantage of new material.** During this parenting season, you might write a story for a children's magazine called "Moving to Grandma's House." Or perhaps you'll share your insight with other grandparents in an article called "Mothering Your Grandchildren."

- **Resist the urge to take over the parenting if you're not providing childcare.** I find it much harder to say "Nana has to work" than I did "Mommy needs to work." If my kids (with the grandkids) ever lived with me even temporarily, it would be hard for me to keep remembering that I'm not the grandkids' mother, nor their entertainment committee.

More and more in our struggling economy, adult children are moving home for a few weeks or months. If this happens, strive to maintain enough structure so that you can keep writing. If you can—and it *is* possible—you'll enjoy having your family there much more.

Running on Parallel Tracks

Whether you write in ten-minute segments between interruptions, or you have an entire day free before your family comes home for supper, your life runs on two tracks: the *writing track* and the *other world track*. These two lives enrich each other, and they're both equally worthy of your undivided attention.

So . . . do you have to be a split personality to handle this? Some days it feels like that! As best-selling Pulitzer Prize-winning novelist Anne Tyler once said:

> *"I've spent so long erecting partitions around the part of me that writes—learning how to close the door on it when ordinary life intervenes, how to close the door on ordinary life when it's time to start writing again—that I'm not sure I could fit the two parts of me back together now."*

Changing Gears

Most writers need some kind of transitional activity to move smoothly from one world to the other. Of course, if you're writing in the midst of babies and toddlers, there's precious little time for transitioning. When my children were small, the transitioning had to take place in my mind as I traveled from the nursery to my closet-turned-office. I had to create a mental picture of the next part of my story on the way there so that when I reached my typewriter, I could type steadily for the ten or fifteen minutes available to me.

Any of this can be accompanied by tea or cocoa to ease you into the writing world.

If you have more time, transitional activities or rituals are lovely. You can go for a walk and let your writing project fill your head space. Before you turn to your writing, you might transition by reading fifteen minutes in a book set in your story's locale. You might like to journal about your characters or your upcoming day's work.

Tuning In and Tuning Out

Both your real life and your writing life demand—and deserve—your total concentration. You need to find some "tricks" to help you change gears. One thing that helps me personally is that my husband calls before he leaves work, so I know when I have just twenty minutes of quiet time left. I can start making the transition to family time before he walks in the door. I used to do the same thing when I knew it was only fifteen minutes until the school bus was due.

A writer's life does run on parallel tracks, and we don't want the train to derail. We need to be able to concentrate on both rails at appropriate times and move smoothly between them. With enough practice, you can do this almost seamlessly. Soon you'll be moving back and forth between your "two lives" without even thinking about it.

Cherish the Commonplace

When I started writing, I gathered nothing but rejection slips as long as I tried to write about fantastic things I had never experienced. I was always hunting for the "extraordinary" idea. I found some—in the newspaper, on TV, or in magazines. I worked hard to turn them into stories and articles, but not a single one of them ever sold. I gathered thirty-plus rejection slips instead.

However, a year after I stopped doing that, I had sold six manuscripts. What changed?

> **Down to Earth**
> My writing career took off when I decided to write about things I experienced (and that really mattered to me) while raising my babies on an Iowa farm. I wrote for children's magazines and family magazines about fixing healthy snacks, about children who couldn't sleep, about hospital helpers when my baby daughter was sick, about the teasing when my oldest daughter got braces, about kids playing house in the corn crib . . .

Nothing extraordinary or earth-shaking. But those simple stories and articles were easy pieces to write, and shockingly easy to sell, most often on the first submission.

Can "Commonplace" Sell?
I honestly couldn't understand it—until I read a page in *Walking on Alligators: a Book of Meditations for Writers* by Susan Shaughnessy.

In part, she wrote:

> "Two-headed calves and bearded ladies are the stuff of carnivals and supermarket tabloids. There is nothing wrong with being diverted by the extraordinary.
>
> But the extraordinary, strangely enough, has no real staying power. We couldn't read about it or view shows about it day after day. It would soon grow dull and distasteful.
>
> The commonplace has more enduring interest. Ordinary daily life, as we know it to really be, makes for absorbing writing that never tires us."

I have found that to be true over time—both as a reader and as a writer.

Your *Real* World

So, if you're worried that you don't live a life that's interesting enough for a writer, think again. Real life—embodied in the authentic people and setting details all around you—truly does interest others.

Cherish the commonplace in your writing. It will resonate with people because it's *real*.

Your Writing Life

Please remember that writing success is not about how much talent you have. And it's not about who you know in publishing. It's about learning and growing—and mostly, *not quitting*. I hope these down-to-earth, personal slices from my own writing life will help you realize that we writers are all alike. We face the same challenges. We have the same dream. You have the power to create your own writing life. My best wishes go with you as you do.

Books by Kristi Holl

SERIES

The Boarding School Mysteries   Zonderkidz/Faithgirlz
Vanished
Betrayed
Burned
Poisoned

Devotionals   Zonderkidz/Faithgirlz
Finding God in Tough Times
What's a Girl to Do?
Shine On, Girl!
Girlz Rock
Chick Chat
No Boys Allowed

TodaysGirls.com   Thomas Nelson
4Give & 4Get
Fun E-Farm
Tangled Web
Chat Freak

Carousel Mysteries   Mid-Praire Books
Deadly Disguise
Stage Fright
A Spin Out of Control

"Julie McGregor"   Standard Publishing
A Change of Heart
A Tangled Web
Two of a Kind
Trusting in the Dark

SINGLE TITLES

More Writer's First Aid: Getting the Writing Done   Writer's Institute Pub.
   Writer's First Aid

Danger at Hanging Rock   David C. Cook Publishers

Hidden in the Fog   Atheneum Books for Children
No Strings Attached
Patchwork Summer
The Haunting of Cabin 13
First Things First
Cast a Single Shadow
Perfect or Not, Here I Come
The Rose Beyond the Wall
Footprints Up My Back
Mystery by Mail
Just Like a Real Family

For Every Joy That Passes   Royal Fireworks Press
Invisible Alex

OTHER BOOKS

Argh! Stegosaurus The Clever Factory
Chomp! Apatosaurus
Grrr! Triceratops
Vegetable Gardening
Devotions for Girls

BLOG

Writer's First Aid: A Medicine Chest of Hope
   http://institutechildrenslit.net/Writers-First-Aid-blog/

Books for Inspiration

Bayles, David, and Ted Orland. *Art & Fear: Observations on the Perils (and Rewards) of Artmaking*

Berg, Elizabeth. *Escaping into the Open*

Brown-Burmeister, and Susan, Linda B. Swanson-Davis, ed., *Glimmer Train Guide to Writing Fiction. Volume 2: Inspiration and Discipline*

Cameron, Julia. *The Artist's Way*
  The Right to Write

Canfield, Jack. *The Success Principles*

Carlson, Richard. *Don't Worry, Make Money*

DeSalvo, Louise, Ph.D. *Writing as a Way of Healing*

Eble, Diane. *Behind the Stories*

Fiore, Neil, Ph.D. *The Now Habit: A Strategic Program for Overcoming Procrastination and Enjoying Guilt-Free Play*

Gann, Judy. *The God of All Comfort: Devotions of Hope for Those Who Chronically Suffer*

Gerard, Phillip. *Writing a Book That Makes a Difference*

Honore, Carl. *In Praise of Slowness: Challenging the Cult of Speed*

Jacobs, Beth. *Writing for Emotional Balance: A Guided Journal to Help You Manage Your Overwhelming Emotions*

Jeffers, Susan. *Feel the Fear and Do It Anyway*

Katz, Christina. *Writer Mama: How To Raise a Writing Career Alongside Your Kids*

Keyes, Ralph. *The Courage to Write*
  The Writer's Book of Hope

King, Stephen. *On Writing*

Kinkade, Thomas. *Lightposts for Living*

Lamott, Ann. *Bird by Bird*

Maisel, Eric. *Deep Writing*
  Fearless Creating

Rottman, Carol, J. Ph.D. *Writers in the Spirit*

Shaughnessy, Susan. *Walking on Alligators: A Book of Meditations for Writers*

Shaw, Benard. *The Guide to Writers' Conferences and Workshops* www.shawguides.com/

Shimberg, Elaine Fantle. *Write Where You Live: Successful Freelancing at Home*

Simon, Rachel. *The Writer's Survival Guide*

Sinetar, Marsha. *Do What You Love, The Money Will Follow*

Webb, Joan C. *The Relief of Imperfection*

Wolf, Anthony, E. *"Get Out of My Life, But First Could You Drive Me and Cheryl to the Mall?": A Parent's Guide to the New Teenager*

Index